SAVING LIVES.
SAVING DIGNITY.

*A Unique End-of-Life Perspective
From Two Emergency Physicians*

ROBERT SHAPIRO, M.D.
and
ALAN MOLK, M.D.

DEDICATION

To our families, friends, and patients,
who have taught us so much about life and death.
Your legacies live on.

Kindness Publishing
Phoenix, AZ 85050
kindnesspublishing@gmail.com

Printed in the United States of America

Cover and Chapter Head Designs by William Love

Book Design by WORD**ART**, LLC West Des Moines, IA

TABLE OF CONTENTS

Introduction

ACKNOWLEDGMENTS

A special word of thanks to our original editor, Rachel Skolnik Light. Our gratitude to Rachel cannot be overemphasized. Without her amazing talents this book would still be merely "pie-in-the-sky." We are indebted to her for making this book a reality.

Additionally, huge kudos to Bill and Lona Love who helped with a second edit as well as designing the book and assisting with self-publishing.

Also, thanks to Ariel Molk (daughter of Dr. Molk) for proof-reading the book.

INTRODUCTION

Most people view Emergency Room (ER) doctors as busy professionals running around saving lives. Unfortunately, saving lives is not always possible. When it is not possible, patients and their families are often unprepared to make end-of-life decisions. They have either never considered the possibility of death, or their physician has never discussed it with them. This book aims to encourage discussions regarding end of life and enable thoughtful, well informed, and compassionate decision making when end of life comes.

As ER doctors, we know both personally and professionally how challenging end-of-life decisions can be. Our own family members have struggled with incurable diseases and we have wrestled with what to do next. As Emergency Physicians, we have practiced for more than 35 years each. Our personal experiences, combined with our training and encounters in the ER, have taught us a lot about death and dying. This book is an effort to share some of these lessons with you, summarizing essential information on the end of life that we feel is essential in helping prepare for that eventuality.

We hope that you find it educational, helpful, and enlightening. Where relevant and illustrative, we have included real-life stories from the ER. The names and identifying information of patients and their families have been changed to protect their privacy. These individuals and their unique stories exemplify patients all over the United States with one thing in common: They came to the ER at the end of their lives.

Our main objective is to make death as dignified, humane, and comfortable as possible. Emergency Physicians are trained to resuscitate patients and sustain lives. In doing so, we have often witnessed modern medical technology cost countless patients a peaceful ending to their lives. When saving lives is not possible, we believe our duty is to help make a patient's final hours and eventual death a dignified, serene, and gracious life event—both for the patient and for their loved ones.

We passionately believe that heroic measures (measures taken as a last resort without which death is certain) are not always the best course of action. When our bodies reach pre-terminal and terminal disease states, heroic measures often lead patients to spend the last moments, hours, days or weeks of their lives in the intensive care unit (ICU) with multiple complex, expensive medications, connected to an array of staff-involved medical devices. These include invasive intravenous lines, beeping monitors, and tubes inserted in various body orifices. Respirators (breathing machines) often restrict patients from communicating with their families, due to the machine itself and also a significant degree of sedation. Many times the patient ultimately dies of either the primary disease or manifestations of the medical process while remaining in the ICU. There is definitely a time and place for heroics, but if the patient is already at or close to the end of life, then these measures are, in our opinion, anything but heroic.

This belief and our own personal and professional experiences have inspired us to have this conversation on the end of life with you. Medicare will cover the cost of such a conversation between the doctor and the patient (at the patient's request),[1] and we hope that similar conversations will take place all over the country. It is our desire that more and more people will begin to see the ER as an environment to begin compassionate palliative or hospice care and not just aggressive, invasive, and all too often, futile care.

We are proud to be part of a growing movement among doctors and other medical professionals addressing this sensitive topic. At the same time, we acknowledge that some people may disagree with our views for intellectual, medical, ethical, moral, religious and/or legal reasons. We also recognize and respect autonomy in medical decision-making and the right of a patient to decline and/or refuse a physician's recommendations and advice. In any case, we hope you find this book valuable and are grateful that you have allowed us to be a part of this conversation.

Before moving forward, we want you to know a little bit about us and the personal experiences that led us to write this book.

DR. MOLK'S STORY

When Love is Letting Go:
A Personal Note from Dr. Molk

In 1977, I emigrated to the United States from South Africa. The decision to do so was largely made for me by my late father, Lazar Molk. He absolutely insisted that I go to the United States to further my medical career and to find a new life. Many people emigrated from South Africa during that time as the social, racial, and political situation was becoming more troublesome and uncertain during the Apartheid years.

At 25 years old, his words to me were unforgettable: "I want you to go to America, even if it means I never get to see you again." I recall being completely blown away by his words at the time, and remain blown away to this day, more than three decades after his passing. How much did my father love me? My father loved me enough to say goodbye and to set me free at his own painful expense and loss.

He knew he had to do what was best for me, even though he would grieve daily about his beloved son being on a different continent and in a different hemisphere. Fortunately, I did get to see him on a few occasions both here in the US and in Africa before his death from pancreatic cancer in 1987. He was so proud and so joyful at the fact that I was happy and had become well established in the USA.

Why do I tell this story? Sometimes saying goodbye is truly the greatest act of love and selflessness.

The "Crystal Ball Epiphany":
Another Personal Note from Dr. Molk

My mother, Sarona Molk, was undoubtedly my greatest role model in life. She was a vivacious 75-year-old before Alzheimer's Dementia set in. I have never known a more loving, benevolent, and delightful human being. The experience of witnessing her descent into Alzheimer's disease was excruciating for me. It reminded me of how poorly we in America deal with incurable and progressive illnesses, end-of-life issues, and the loss of dignity associated with these events. Her six-year downward spiral with this dreadful disease was an ongoing learning experience that stirred my interest and passion in end-of-life issues.

I often painfully recall my visits to my beloved mother during her final year or so in the Alzheimer's unit. Every time that I drove over to see her and take her out for ice cream or to pick up a few things at the supermarket whilst pushing her in a wheelchair, I would feel a recurrent sense of sadness and hopelessness—every time felt like a punch in the gut. I dreaded seeing her in that downward spiral. One day as I sat across from her as she was staring into space, incontinent and in diapers, unable to feed or wash herself, without the ability to speak and not knowing who I was, I had an epiphany:

In my mind, I turned back the clock about six or seven years before Alzheimer's had affected her so profoundly. I imagined myself sitting next to my mother laughing and having fun and holding a crystal ball in my hands. I then imagined myself getting serious for a moment and having my mother look into the crystal ball. I imagined stating, "Mom, I'm sorry to tell you this, but this is what you are going to look and be like seven years from now."

What would she have said? As someone who truly valued her dignity, her appearance and independence, her self-pride, and her amazing interpersonal skills, she undoubtedly would have said: "Oh no! Please don't let that happen to me! If it does, please push me off a cliff!" She would never, ever have wanted to continue living in the state she was in. At that moment, it became abundantly clear to me that many, if not most, people who have suffered or are suffering a similar terminal fate might feel exactly the way she would have.

DR. SHAPIRO'S STORY

In 1987, my wife, Kristine Flanagan, was stricken with brain cancer at the age of 27. After two years of stormy ups and downs, with long periods of improvement (which allowed us to spend time together and with our infant children), it became clear one night that she was going to die very soon. She was admitted to the hospital, and, when she got there, her doctor asked whether or not to resuscitate her, should the need arise. I was faced with the same decision many families face—yet I was very aware of what the outcome would likely be. I was able to talk with her attending internist, who advised against it. I made the decision to not intubate or resuscitate.

CHAPTER 1

Making the Case for Doing Things Differently

The Safety Net

Almost everyone has had the good fortune (often misfortune) of visiting an Emergency Room (ER), or, as we prefer to call it, the Emergency Department (ED). Perhaps your child woke up with a fever, an earache, or croup in the middle of the night. Maybe your grandmother fell and broke her hip. Maybe your dad developed crushing chest pain and had a heart attack, or your friend had food poisoning and was getting weak and dehydrated. Or maybe it was you, the reader, having a miscarriage or experiencing excruciating pain from a kidney stone. The medical reasons for going to the ER are endless and cover the entire spectrum of medical illnesses and injuries.

The ER and its staff represent the ultimate safety net of the American health care system. We are open 24 hours a day, seven days a week, 365 days a year. Unlike other medical specialists, no appointment is ever needed. You can show up to any ER at any time and expect to be evaluated. As ER providers (doctors, PAs, and nurse practitioners), we are required by law to see, evaluate, and stabilize any patient who walks through the door. By federal law, you cannot be turned away from an ER, no matter your ability to pay or your insurance status. You will be billed for services, which are not cheap, but you can and must be seen by an ER doctor. This is true even for a cold, a stubbed toe, or a hangnail. You will be medically examined, evaluated, and stabilized. Failure to do so can result in a fine of the ER physician of up to $50,000 that is not covered by our malpractice insurance.

The ER is typically a crazy and hectic environment where organized chaos is the rule. A busy ER might have 60 patients and 20 more in the waiting room, simultaneously. Nobody has appointments and many arrive by ambulance. Patients' diseases, complaints, and injuries run the gamut from obstetrics/gynecology to pediatrics, from trauma to otolaryngology (ENT or ear, nose, and throat), from psychiatry to orthopedics, from neurology to toxicology, and everything in between.

In most instances, we are seeing the patient for the first time and have just one shot to get things right. We have a limited amount of time and handle up to 20 patients, some of whom have medical problems that are difficult to diagnose and treat, at the same time. We are also under tight scrutiny to comply with patient satisfaction goals and many other benchmarks, protocols, and requirements to ensure excellent patient care. To be successful, we must also know risk management (how not to get sued), cost containment (how to limit unnecessary testing and procedures), and throughput (how to take care of patients expeditiously) to minimize long wait times.

The tracking board of any busy ER will show at any time of

the day or night some or all of the following complaints: heavy vaginal bleeding, chest pain, fever, headache, fell off ladder, neck pain, vomiting, abdominal pain, rash, abscess, sore throat, weakness, anxiety, suicidal ideation, wheezing, laceration, dislocated shoulder, asthma attack, blood in urine, swollen knee, congestive heart failure, eye drainage, fell off bike, gallbladder attack, burn, alcohol withdrawal, need refill of medications, swollen testicle, toothache, sprained ankle, carbon monoxide exposure, Q-tip in ear, heat exhaustion, allergic reaction, swallowed hearing aid battery, got in fight in bar, dizziness, retained vaginal tampon, seizure, beaten up by boyfriend, high blood sugar, fainting, post-operative complications, etc. In addition, there are the other serious cases we are managing and for which television shows like "ER" portray. These include bad car accidents, stabbings and shootings, heart attacks, strokes, overdoses, and cardiac arrests.

The knowledge base of an ER doctor needs to be very expansive to take care of all our patients' needs. We are proud of our extensive training and experience and pleased to be part of the medical safety net. We take great pride in treating a young child at 3:00 a.m. with an earache or a man with excruciating pain from a kidney stone in the middle of the night. It makes us feel like we make a difference and results in enormous job satisfaction. Moreover, we get an adrenaline rush from working under pressure, like when we are told that an ambulance is five minutes out with an unconscious patient that has heat stroke, took an overdose, or has had a cardiac arrest. We are at our best when time is of the essence.

At the same time, we feel a sense of failure when a patient dies on our watch and often experience intense grief when the death is sudden and unexpected. There is nothing harder than telling a spouse, child, or parent that our resuscitative efforts were unsuccessful and that their loved one has died. We also see the dysfunctional side of medicine and society's ills in the ER on a daily basis. A substantial part of our time each day is spent dealing with patients' personal and social issues. We feel the pain of our patients and their families. At the end of a busy ER shift, we are usually mentally, physically, and often emotionally, drained.

Many ER physicians pay a price for working in the ER, medicine's safety net. Depression, substance, and alcohol abuse can ensue. Burnout is fairly common. Marriages can suffer. We can become unhealthy and have shorter life expectancies. That said, if we begin to feel sorry for ourselves, thinking of one unfortunate patient is usually enough to exit the pity train. In a nutshell, ER doctors are very busy physicians, vigorously diagnosing and treating patients all day and all night and making people feel better. Our job is saving lives.

So, how can two ER doctors believe so strongly in addressing end-of-life issues without unnecessary end-of-life heroics? We believe that, as physicians, our role is to alleviate suffering when death is imminent, not to prolong the inevitable. Although this seems counter-intuitive, it is an idea that is gaining momentum. Our beliefs are consistent with the recent guidelines and recommendations of the American College of Emergency Physicians (ACEP, our own American Medical Association).

These beliefs are referred to in ACEP's "Choosing Wisely" campaign, which promotes "wise decisions about the most appropriate care based on a patient's individual situation."[2] One of the recommendations from this campaign is to identify certain patients in the ER who would benefit from palliative and hospice care and to initiate those referrals directly from the ER. So, although avoiding end-of-life heroics in the ER may seem counter-intuitive in some respects, we are not non-conformists doing our own thing. We strongly embrace this cultural shift in emergency medicine.

Do Everything

We are all guilty of the "do everything" approach. As family and as care givers, it is difficult to make the decision not to "do everything." In 1940, if a 40-year old patient was admitted to the hospital with pneumonia, that patient was put in an oxygen tent and given maintenance fluids and pain medicine. The patient either survived pneumonia or died from it. In today's world, this scenario could play out in multiple ways:

• In Scenario 1, a healthy, 40-year old patient is admitted to the hospital with pneumonia. The patient is placed on intravenous antibiotics, improves and is discharged.

• In Scenario 2, the same patient is admitted to the hospital with pneumonia. The patient's condition deteriorates despite intravenous antibiotics and respiratory treatments. The patient is transferred to the Intensive Care Unit (ICU), placed on mechanical ventilation, and ultimately survives to hospital discharge.

• In Scenario 3, the same patient is admitted to the hospital with pneumonia. The patient's condition deteriorates despite intravenous antibiotics, respiratory treatments, transfer to the ICU, and mechanical ventilation. The patient develops Acute Respiratory Distress Syndrome (ARDS), is given multiple medications to maintain blood pressure, develops Multiple Organ Dysfunction Syndrome (MODS) and dies.

Most reasonable people would agree that, in this case, everything should be attempted for the otherwise young and healthy patient.

Now, let's consider a different scenario. In 1940, if a

75-year-old female with progressive metastatic cancer was admitted to the hospital, she was made as comfortable as possible with pain medication and oxygen and died. Let's imagine that same patient is admitted to the hospital, through the ER, today. Because of respiratory distress, and at the request of her family, the patient is put on mechanical ventilation and transferred to the ICU where her condition continues to deteriorate. She is unable to talk with her family because she is on a ventilator and requires strong intravenous sedation to tolerate it. She spends the last one to two weeks of her life in the ICU, and, in spite of maximum treatment, develops MODS (Multiple Organ Dysfunction Syndrome) and dies.

In this scenario, the patient's ultimate demise is fairly predictable in advance. This example illustrates how medical technology —although greatly advanced since 1940—may not truly provide benefits to a patient at the end of life.

So, why do we default to "do everything?" Is this decision really in the patient's best interest? Most of us simply cannot accept the fact that life eventually comes to an end. Doctors frequently see death as "the ultimate enemy." This is typically especially true for ER doctors. If you are our patient in the ER, we will try to keep you alive no matter what. Many other specialists have a similar "never give up" approach. Some nephrologists (kidney specialists) will find a reason to keep you on dialysis, as they know that death will ensue shortly after stopping dialysis. Oncologists will often try another round of chemotherapy—even when the prognosis is gloomy and the patient is tired and suffering with terminal cancer. Similarly, cardiologists will sometimes attempt all kinds of fancy technology in patients who are near death, just because the technology is available. We hate "giving up."

The above are just a few examples of how we physicians are a large part of the problem in dealing with end-of-life issues. We refuse to give up even when we know that some of our treatments are likely futile and only prolong patients' agony. We refuse to give up even when we know that many of these patients have a quality of life that we would find unacceptable. In fact, a recent survey shows just this.[3] When over 1,000 physicians across the USA were asked whether they would want to be "DNRs" (Do Not Resuscitate) if faced with a terminal illness, 88% said yes. Only 12% wanted "everything done."[3] This is an appalling double standard.

We ourselves are in denial. We turn a blind eye to the atrocious loss of dignity our patients endure in their end-of-life states because we are determined to keep our treatments going no matter what. Even worse, we often give patients and their families false hope of recovery and improvement. We never do this intentionally, but we hate to look like quitters or failures.

Part of the need for physicians to "do everything" stems from the paranoia of being sued by patients, or more likely, by family members for "abandoning" or "denying care." The legal world, as you know, is murky and complex. We violate our own golden rule of "do for the patient what you would do for yourself and your own family." Patients and their families are also a colossal part of the problem due to their refusal and/or inability to cope with death even when death is imminent and inevitable. We hope that this book will help people understand and deal with these issues, so that end-of-life decisions can be made in a more objective way.

Saying Goodbye

Death can come unexpectedly and suddenly in the form of a massive stroke or heart attack, a massive blood clot to the lungs (pulmonary embolus), or by a myriad of different fatal traumatic injuries. Strange as it may seem, many people believe that sudden death is "not a bad way to go." There is something morbidly appealing about the idea that "he never knew what hit him " and that the end was fast. Don't believe us? Just ask some of your older friends and relatives.

With sudden death, the deceased does not suffer long— maybe for seconds, minutes, or a few days. The real sufferers are their loved ones who had no chance to prepare, to say goodbye, or to make peace. There is often "unfinished business" and unre-solved issues. For many families, emotional recovery is extremely difficult and often incomplete.

Expected and gradual death is a totally different story. There is time to prepare, provided that you are not in denial. When the end comes, there is usually some sense of relief that accompanies the grief because the suffering has ended for both the patient and for their loved ones. Statistically, you will succumb to expected death rather than sudden death. Therefore, we encourage you to start thinking about end of life and preparing for it. When we see a patient in the ER with an end-stage or terminal illness and their family who chose hospice care, we often see rational thought, courage, acceptance, serenity and love. In contrast, we often see desperation, turmoil, restlessness and frustration when people decline hospice and opt for more aggressive treatment.

Let's consider for a moment how we handle terminally ill pets. We know pets aren't people but for a lot of us, they are beloved family members. Rationally, we know that at some time we will have to deal with a pet's end of life. We do not want our pets to suffer because we love them. As a result, sometimes we make the painful decision to say goodbye and euthanize them. Losing a family pet is painful, heart wrenching, and leaves a gaping emptiness in our lives, but we accept it and we move on.

Similarly, when our children graduate from high school, for most, an era ends. They find jobs or go to college and we are left with an empty nest. We learn to accept that and we begin a new chapter in our lives. We have to let our kids go, so they can become competent and independent adults. It's time to say goodbye. However difficult it is to accept, saying goodbye is one of life's inevitabilities.

When it comes to loved ones who are terminally ill, there seems to be a different approach. All too frequently, families are in denial either because they cannot or do not want to face reality. They simply cannot say goodbye. There are lots of reasons for this: unresolved personal issues, immense fear of losing the loved one, the thought of life without that loved one, and abandonment issues, to name just a few. Whatever the reason, denial, unfortunately, often prolongs suffering.

Here are a few real-life examples of what happens when we can't say goodbye: An acquaintance lost his mother a few years ago. She was in her 80s. She had advanced cancer, as well as other medical problems. She was in constant pain and looked terrible. All she wanted from her two children was "permission to go." She was tired and "ready to meet her Maker." Her son and his sister insisted she keep fighting, not "give up," and undergo more chemotherapy, which she had tolerated poorly and made her last days miserable. Neither of them could bear the thought of her dying, irrespective of how awful she looked and felt.

Two additional and somewhat typical patient encounters further illustrate what happens when we can't let go: The first was a 20-year-old who was born with cerebral palsy, profound mental retardation, and seizures. Amazingly, he made it to 20 years of age but he required total care. Unable to feed himself, he received daily nourishment through a feeding tube in his stomach. He was permanently rigid and spastic. He was incontinent and in diapers. His mother was his caregiver and Power of Attorney. His dad was not in the picture. He never walked and was confined to bed or a wheelchair. He never talked or communicated, except to cry out when it was thought that he was in pain. He frequently got pneumonia from aspirating (food and liquids getting in his lungs) and required prolonged hospitalizations with massive doses of antibiotics only to return home to his vegetative state.

On the day he came to the ER, he had suffered yet another bout of aspiration pneumonia. He looked awful. His temperature was 104.5 degrees F, he was struggling to breathe, and had low oxygen saturations in the 70s (normal is over 94%). Fortunately, we got an IV in him to obtain blood work and infuse IV fluids and antibiotics. His chest x-ray looked extremely bad with pneumonia present in both lungs. Initially, he improved for a short time and his oxygen levels were slightly better. However, after an hour or so, even with massive doses of antibiotics, he took a turn for the worse. We told his mother that his prognosis was grim, that he had septicemia (blood infection), and was in respiratory failure. We felt he needed comfort care. We did ask about her wishes regarding whether or not to place him on a respirator, which is a very standard question when a patient is clearly in respiratory failure.. We were hoping she was ready to say goodbye, but instead she insisted that we put a tube down his throat and place him on a respirator. We had no choice but to follow her wishes. He was put on a respirator and placed in the ICU where further aggressive treatment was instituted. Despite these efforts, he died 24 hours later. Had he survived, he would have been back to his previous tragic and pitiful state, only to return to the ER in the future under similar circumstances. Instead of dying peacefully at home surrounded by loved ones—the way the vast majority of us would prefer—he died in a gloomy ICU.

Another patient was a young lady in her twenties with a tragic diagnosis of metastatic sarcoma (a malignant tumor of the connective tissue that has spread) that failed to respond to any form of radiation or chemotherapy. She was transported to the ER by ambulance, unresponsive, and barely breathing. Death was imminent. The ambulance brought her to the ER because a family member called 911, citing that she was unresponsive. Fortunately, one of the EMS crew noted some papers in the home and brought them to the ER. Those documents included an advanced directive, signed recently by the patient herself, stating that she wanted no further treatment in the event of a cardiac or respiratory arrest. She did not wish for CPR (cardiopulmonary resuscitation) or a respirator.

Seconds later, the same family member who had called 911 arrived, got in the doctor's face and yelled, "Why the hell are you not doing chest compressions?" The doctor, doing everything to maintain his composure, calmly replied, "She is dying and does not want any heroic measures, and I need to respect her wishes." Security was on standby, as this family member's body language was hostile and aggressive. The patient quietly died in about ten minutes and the enraged family member broke down crying. The family member was comforted by hospital staff and the chaplain. His grieving process had begun. In this example, the patient's wishes were respected and she was allowed a dignified, natural death.

Hospital and ICU Admission

Patients and/or family members often say things like: "I'd like to be admitted to the hospital" or "I think my Mom should be admitted for a few days to rest," or "I can't take him home in this condition. He needs to stay in the hospital" or "We want Dad admitted for more tests." Many of these patient/family requests are reasonable. Many are not.

Those who want to be admitted "to get some rest" are in for a rude awakening. Rest? In a hospital? This is definitely a myth. Let us provide a reality check. During the average day, an inpatient has his vital signs (pulse, blood pressure, respiratory rate) taken several times, has numerous visits from nurses and other health care professionals, gets blood work, x-rays/CT scans/MRIs, among other procedures and interruptions. They are often awakened during the night and may be subjected to a lot of ambient noise. This does not create "a relaxing holiday". Patients also get unpleasant surprises when their insurance or health plan refuses to cover what is deemed "an unnecessary hospital admission."

Inpatient admission (or ICU in the event of a severe condition) does benefit a patient with a reversible, curable, treatable, or manageable condition that cannot be adequately treated at home or in the outpatient setting. In addition, some patients need to stay in the hospital when a potentially life-threatening, reversible, curable, or manageable condition could develop within 6-24 hours. Since an exact diagnosis cannot always be made in the ER, a patient's condition may deteriorate and require urgent intervention. In this case, many times the patient is temporarily placed in the hospital for precautionary measures and close observation .

Hospital treatment, including surgery, can have unintended consequences. Medical errors and mistakes that result in disability, tragedy, or death do happen. These unintended consequences are especially common in the elderly and can include development of confusion and disorientation. This is particularly frequent in people who already have memory impairment or early dementia. It is very upsetting for patients and their loved ones and the condition can be exacerbated by ICU admission. The term "ICU psychosis" is a well-described medical concept and describes how some patients in the ICU are "put over the edge" mentally. They become very agitated, confused, disruptive, and even violent. They often need heavy sedation or restraints to prevent injury to themselves and others.

Fortunately, hospitals across the country recognize these potential hazards and have placed many protocols, initiatives, and systems in place in an effort to ensure patient safety. Nonetheless, the reality is that some patients truly do not benefit from admission to a medical/surgical unit or ICU. We as physicians have learned, and can now predict with surprising accuracy, which patients can safely return to the comforts of their own homes. Hospital stays are at times ineffective, extremely costly, and potentially harmful.

ICU admission makes a difference for patients with treatable, reversible, or curable conditions who need highly sophisticated and complex treatments and monitoring. However, admitting patients with multiple organ disease and/or failure and those who are near death yields expectedly disappointing and poor results. To put it bluntly, these patients are high cost and high maintenance but very low yield. Fear of being sued often puts undue pressure on the physician, twisting his/her arm to admit patients to the ICU and to "do everything possible."

Similar concerns apply to inpatient elective surgeries in older patients or to patients with serious underlying medical problems, like heart disease, emphysema, or kidney failure. Take this real life example: A friend discovered that his elderly mother had a thoracic aortic aneurysm (an abnormally stretched and weakened section of the aorta , the main blood vessel in the chest and abdomen). This was found on a chest x-ray taken because of a bad cough; her doctor ordered the chest x-ray to be sure that it was not pneumonia. The aneurysm was an incidental finding. She had no symptoms from it and was otherwise a sprightly octogenarian. Such an aneurysm grows gradually over time and can rupture if the person lives long enough. Once it ruptures, death follows very quickly. There was no way of knowing when this could happen. Maybe it would be months, maybe years.

After consulting with various specialists and at the insistence of her family, the friend and his mother decided she should have the aneurysm repaired. Given that she was in her 80s, this was a highly risky and complex operation that required her to go to a very specialized, out-of-state facility. She survived the four-hour operation, but she had an extremely difficult time post-operatively and was in the ICU for days. She became confused and combative during her hospitalization, but she eventually recovered enough to go home. However, she was never the same person; she appeared more physically frail and less mentally sharp. Less than three weeks later, her son found her dead on the floor of her apartment when he went to pick her up for their weekly lunch date. Her cause of death was deemed "natural." He subsequently told me how he regretted "putting his poor mother through this."

Obviously, hindsight is 20/20, but this is one of innumerable cases where aggressive treatment may not have been the better choice. Clearly, choosing between aggressive and conservative treatment is tough and can go either way; we must always consider the options and likely outcomes. That being said, it is important to remember that sometimes, less is more.

Futile Care

Futile aggressive medical care is when it is evident to doctors and nurses that a patient has a disease or diseases that is/are either untreatable or unmanageable, even with the most up-to-date medical knowledge and resources. We as health care providers have to acknowledge that a terminal state is imminent and that aggressive treatment will not change the course of the illness.

In some scenarios, the picture may not initially be clear and other variables (including an occasional miracle) may come into play. Medicine is not an exact science , and exceptions to the rule do occasionally occur. That said, we are pretty good at recognizing end-of-life situations. Most non-doctors are pretty good at it too. Comments like, "He looks like death" or "I've seen bodies at a viewing that look better than him" all indicate that even people with little medical knowledge can recognize impending death. Nonetheless, refusal to quit, fears of loss, fear of litigation, and inability to recognize medicine's limitations often lead us to aggressively treat or admit patients.

To illustrate this point, let's recall the case we presented earlier of a 20-year-old that occupied an ICU bed for 24 hours. Fortunately, there was no ICU bed shortage that day. When an ICU is full, often one or more patients in the ER who are seriously or critically ill—patients that are very likely to benefit from ICU care do not get an ICU bed. In other words, a terminally ill patient occupying an ICU bed may prevent a patient who truly needs and can actually benefit from ICU treatment getting an ICU bed. This happens all too often and simply is not right.

Only fairly recently, with the realization that we do not have endless dollars for health care, has this become a hot topic. Critical care specialists and the medical literature acknowledge there is a problem and have shown great intellectual honesty by beginning to address this topic. Things are changing. Deferring costly and futile care for those with an extremely poor prognosis and treating them in a non-hospital setting is becoming more common. More and more physicians are not automatically accepting all terminally ill patients for hospital based care. This is gratifying, given that most of their training and livelihood is based on aggressive and highly sophisticated treatments. Having the humility, understanding, and acceptance to admit that they cannot cure all is so important whilst simultaneously becoming more enlightened about the value of palliative and hospice care. Many of these difficult and controversial hospital and ICU dilemmas can be averted; calmness, tranquility, and dignity can prevail with proper advanced planning. The cost of hospital and ICU care is astronomical, and we should spare no expense to save lives. However, we should not be using inpatient and ICU treatment for futile care.

Staggering Costs

Human life is precious, but so is dignity. As discussed earlier, many people are in denial about death. They like to believe they will live forever or just don't want to think or talk about their own mortality. Consequently, when death appears real or imminent, they fight it at all costs.

So, what does it cost? The answer is: A lot. It is no secret that there is a health care crisis in America. We have the dubious distinction of spending a disproportionate number of health dollars per capita compared to other high-income nations. According to a 2013 study: "Despite spending more on health care, Americans had poor health outcomes, including shorter life expectancy and greater prevalence of chronic conditions." In 2014, health expenditures in the U.S. were $9,523 per capita, representing 17.5% of Gross Domestic Product.[6]

There are several diseases that have been caused by the technology that keeps people alive in the Intensive Care Unit. These are known as diseases of medical progress and include: MODS (Multiple Organ Dysfunction Syndrome), sepsis or SIRS (Systemic Inflammatory Response Syndrome) and hospital-acquired, nosocomial infections. MODS is a series of organ failures as the patient's condition progresses in the ICU. Failure of one system interacts with the failure of the second and third until death may become inevitable. When four or more vital organs have failed, mortality rates increase to over 80%. SIRS, or "sepsis," is a situation in which a patient's response to a stress—usually an infection—causes damage to the patient. It is characterized by a decrease in oxygenation to the organs and results in a loss of function. Nosocomial infections are infections often unique to the hospital environment. In the hospital, organisms develop extreme resistance to antibiotics due to their extensive use. These diseases of medical progress have an enormous impact on the clinical course of patients whose illness requires admission to a hospital or ICU.

Now, let's talk about the elephant in the room: The grossly disproportionate amount of health dollars spent in the last few months of life. The approximations are staggering; 25-30% of Medicare health care dollars are spent in the last year of life.[7] This is astounding, especially considering how much is spent on futile, aggressive, and invasive treatments that do not prolong life or improve outcomes. In fact, often they only prolong suffering at the expense of human dignity. We believe this is wrong, inhumane, and irresponsible, since many end-of-life decisions contribute to sky-rocketing health care costs.

Fortunately, a shift in how we deal with end-of-life issues is coming for U.S. health care providers. Some of this is driven by the fact that we simply cannot afford to continue with futile treatments at the late stages of an illness. Medicare is now denying payment to hospitals for patients readmitted to the hospital within 30 days for many common medical conditions. The government realizes that we are facing a serious financial problem and that the current system is not sustainable.

Hospitals are looking for creative ways to deal with this problem. There is a strong shift towards home-based care, including visiting nurses, telemedicine, and many outpatient programs. These cost-saving measures are becoming a rapidly-growing industry. Fortunately, outpatient palliative care and hospice care for those with end-of-life diseases and serious conditions are also being utilized more. We strongly support these programs because one of their most beautiful objectives is maintaining human dignity.

The Struggle

Embracing and implementing palliative and hospice care as well as end-of-life issues is an uphill battle. Both physicians and the public face a number of hurdles. Although ER doctors have become increasingly aware of the need for dignified end-of-life care, we also face obstacles to addressing these needs on a daily basis.

Let's first discuss why it is difficult to educate the lay public: To accept, understand, and be receptive to end-of-life matters requires the ability to acknowledge mortality. As long as denial and the need to cling to life at all costs are present, the barriers are formidable. Combined with the notion that doctors can miraculously cure even the sickest patient, those barriers are even more daunting. Now add in unfamiliarity with palliative and hospice care options and a dose of paranoia. It is very clear that enlightening the lay public is a huge challenge.

That said, physicians are also a major part of the problem for a variety of reasons, including:

• Lack of familiarity: Although hard to believe, many physicians have not had formal training in end-of-life care. Postgraduate medical training to include a fellowship in Palliative and Hospice Care is available but only a small number of physicians have actually had this training. Historically, there has been little formal training in these areas in medical school or residency, although this is changing.

• Lack of time: In a busy ER on a busy day, having the conversation with patients and families about end-of-life issues can be very difficult, if not impossible. Sick and not-so-sick patients are impatient and want to be seen right away. Many do not have a bona fide emergency, but to them their problem is an emergency. Office-based doctors may tell you the same story. The vast majority of them are very busy and caught up in seeing patients and doing all kinds of procedures and operations. Paper work and practice administration are also very time consuming.

• Having the conversation about end-of-life options is not seen as "our job."

• Fear of litigation: Doctors fear that if they do not go to all extremes with a patient who has a terminal illness, the patient's family may get a lawyer and sue.

• A culture change is needed, and change is hard: We default to treating aggressively even when it is clear that a patient is near death. As discussed earlier, we are wired this way.

• Education is key, but this takes time, money, and effort. Additionally, the following is a brief summary and incomplete list of examples of challenges that ER doctors face on a daily basis that put additional pressure on us and limit our time to have conversations with families about their end-of-life wishes. Length of Stay (LOS): How long does the patient stay in the ER for evaluation/testing and treatment from arrival to admission or discharge? How long is the hospital stay as compared to national averages?

• Numerous core measures, initiatives, benchmarks, and protocols, most of which are about good patient care

• Risk management: Trying to always do the right thing even under extremely challenging conditions

• Cost containment: To not add to the patient's hospital bill by doing unnecessary testing

• Patient satisfaction: All hospitals consider this very important and Medicare reimbursement is partly based on this measure

Very Ill Repeat Patients and the Need for a Plan

Why are we telling you all of this? As Emergency Physicians for more than 35 years each, we have come across just about every disease, condition and injury known in America. Yes, we've seen everything—from common conditions like influenza and sprained ankles, to more serious encounters like heart attacks and meningitis, to a whole slew of rarer conditions. Fortunately, most common conditions/diseases/injuries are treatable and reversible, and have a good prognosis. Other serious common conditions like advanced heart disease, Type I diabetes, stroke, and many forms of cancer have a less favorable prognosis.

There has been a dramatic change in the past 25 years or so

in the type of patients we see in the ER. The patients are older, sicker, and more complex (meaning they often have many different things wrong with them). The reasons for this are well known: People are living longer than before due to an increased emphasis on a healthy lifestyle and the availability of more specialized treatments, such as dialysis for kidney failure, improved treatments/surgeries for cancer and heart disease. Degenerative diseases or diseases of aging (e.g., heart disease, cancer, strokes, arthritis, fractures, osteoporosis, and dementia) are more prevalent.

The typical patient with multiple visits to the ER may be on 15-20 different medications, has a primary care doctor, and has more than one specialist. Many have late stage and serious life-limiting diseases. These patients are sometimes all alone in the world, but others are often accompanied and cared for by their adult child(ren). Here are a few real cases from the ER that fit this picture (the names below have been changed to protect the privacy of patients and their families):

Alicia is only 55 years old and still smokes. She is on disability. She looks about 75 and is very frail. She arrives in the ER because her blood pressure is very elevated at 230/140. She has been unable to keep her routine blood pressure medications down because she has been vomiting for two days. As a result, her blood pressure is dangerously high. She is vomiting because she has gastroparesis (one of numerous serious diabetic complications that causes intermittent vomiting). She is also on dialysis because of kidney failure from diabetes but she feels too ill to go to her dialysis treatment. So, she comes to the ER instead.

Her emphysema is acting up, and she needs a breathing treatment. We use IV medications to lower her blood pressure, but she needs admission for further treatment. She also needs

lots of morphine for pain due to neuropathy, arthritis, and herniated discs. She is a chronic pain patient. Not surprisingly, she is
also depressed and anxious. She has advanced osteoporosis due
to smoking and inactivity. She fell and broke her hip just a few
months prior to this ER visit. Her vision is very compromised due
to diabetic eye complications and the circulation in her legs is poor
from Peripheral Arterial Disease (PAD).

Alicia has many specialists treating her diseases and symptoms. When she is not in the hospital, this unfortunate lady is at
dialysis three times a week for a minimum of three to four hours
and travels from one doctor and physical therapy appointment to
another. She looks unhappy and depressed. Her quality of life is
very poor.

It's unclear how long she will stay alive but she has no advanced
directives and is a "full code." That means that, if she has a cardiac
arrest, "everything should be done to save her." Neither she nor her
husband have any idea as to what "everything" means.

Another example: Claire is only 43, but Multiple Sclerosis
affects her severely. She is bedridden. She has never had a remission. She also has a permanent tracheotomy and a urinary catheter. Her caregiver must wipe her after a bowel movement. She
can barely speak and is in constant pain. She is in and out of the
hospital with recurring pneumonia and urinary tract infections.
The powerful antibiotics she gets are becoming less effective due to
bacterial resistance. She keeps returning to the ER to be admitted.
She now has a fever and a potentially life-threatening infection.
She will probably improve once again and go home, only to return
to her prior helpless state. Her prognosis for recovery or remission
is slim to none and her quality of life borders on tragic.

Another example: Matt is a 68-year-old army veteran who

served in Vietnam. Somewhere along the way, he contracted Hepatitis C. He drank heavily in his youth and now has advanced cirrhosis and liver cancer. He looks extremely ill and is very lethargic as a result of hepatic encephalopathy (his brain has become "poisoned" because his liver is no longer functioning properly). He has developed marked and recurrent ascites (a collection of fluid in the abdomen) and peritonitis (abdominal inflammation and infection), which are known cirrhosis complications. To make him comfortable, he continually returns to the ER to have needles placed in his belly to drain up to eight liters of fluid at a time – an amount equivalent to four large bottles of soda. He also needs IV antibiotics to temporarily clear the infection. There is no cure other than a liver transplant. His wife and son look tired, frustrated, and worn out. They seem to think he is getting a liver transplant soon. Unfortunately, no such thing is on the horizon. When asked whether they appreciate how sick Matt is, his family seems to understand. However, when asked if they are prepared for what will happen if he does not get a liver transplant, they say that none of his liver specialists have prepared them for this possibility. They both get a little teary but are grateful for the reality check. Never has a conversation been held with the liver specialist about the option or eventuality of palliative or hospice care. They are all suffering and need support and alternatives.

These are just a few of thousands of examples of very ill repeat patients to the ER. While not the intention of these patients, they are a huge drain on medical staff resources and dollars and end up being a major burden on the health care system. These patients are complex. They want to live even though they have many serious incurable medical problems. Many conditions can be controlled, stabilized, or "Band-Aided" but these patients will never be healthy again. Many are in pain much of the time. Their chances of living to a ripe old age are slim to none. Their options for cure are severely limited.

You might wonder why a physician would not discuss a patient's prognosis. The truth is, sometimes there is little incentive to do so. These patients generate income and revenue for the physicians involved as long as they are in their care. Other times, providers find the topic too uncomfortable and even taboo. Whatever the reason, having these conversations can be very difficult for medical providers. At the same time, it is absolutely crucial. It's one thing being a patient who still has an acceptable quality of life (as defined by the patient), and this group of patients does exist. It's another thing to be a patient who is suffering and deeply unhappy. Many of these patients are "sick and tired of being sick and tired" with no plan in place to deal with further setbacks or deterioration.

The best way to avoid this situation is prevention and, of course, good genes. Be lucky enough to be born to healthy parents with a history of longevity. Keep fit and maintain a healthy weight, exercise, eat right, don't smoke or do drugs, drink alcohol in moderation, reduce stress, and go for regular checkups and cancer screenings. Sadly, though, regardless of good genes and attention to health, severe illness and disease strike anyway. It's best to have a plan.

Key Issues in the Decision Making Process

Preparing

Most of us spend parts of our days preparing for something. We prepare for the day ahead. We prepare for meetings. We prepare for events, trips, lectures and speeches. Athletes prepare vigorously for competitions and sporting events. Golfers prepare for the Majors, 100-meter sprinters for the Olympic Games, and starting pitchers for the World Series. We also prepare diligently and lovingly for so many of life's precious milestones: birth, religious events, jobs, engagements, weddings, and retirement, among many others. We suggest you prepare for your end of life with the same diligence you would for a sales presentation that could land you a $10M contract. So, how do you do this?

(1) Have advanced directives. Get your will and wishes in order, speak to your spouse/partner and/or other family members, family doctor, your attorney and your spiritual advisor. Don't wait. Do it now.

(2) Consider palliative and hospice care when facing a serious life-limiting illness.

(3) Consider going the route of DNR (Do Not Resuscitate) when faced with a terminal illness. You will prevent unnecessary costs and maintain your dignity.

Being personally responsible about these crucial issues is so important. We pay a terrible price for not preparing for our final life event by unnecessarily burdening our grieving survivors.

Autonomy

It is critically important to recognize that decisions at the end of life should be about the patient's wishes. Often, families insist on treatment that the patient would refuse. The family may have the right to influence the decision and even make the decision when the patient is no longer competent to do so. However, that decision must ultimately reflect the patient's wishes.

Put yourself in the position of the patient: Would you want something done to you because it's in the best interest of others or because it's in your best interest?

Legal Considerations

The law allows us to make decisions in advance regarding the type of medical treatment one might choose. A competent person can delegate someone (known as an agent) to make decisions regarding his/her care using a designated Power of Attorney for Health Care. A competent person can also make their healthcare wishes clear and enforceable with a doctor's help by completion of advanced directives. There are also a small yet growing number of states (California, Montana, Oregon, Washington, and Vermont) which have provided for legal termination of life in certain controlled circumstances. This issue is highly controversial and is not the subject of this book.

Deciding What's Important To You When Receiving End-of-Life Care

In his book, David Kessler lists some things you might want to consider when facing end-of-life. Some of the things you might want to consider include:

- Being treated as a living human being;

- Maintaining a sense of hopefulness;

- Being cared for by those who can maintain a sense of hopefulness;

- Expressing feelings and emotions about death in one's own way;

- Participating in all decisions concerning one's care;

- Being cared for by compassionate, sensitive, knowledgeable people who will attempt to understand the patient's needs;

- Expecting continuing medical care, even though the goals may change from "cure" to "comfort";

- Having all questions answered honestly and fully;

- Seeking spirituality;

- Being free of physical pain;

- Expressing feeling and emotions about pain in one's own way;

- The ability of children to participate in death;

- The ability to understand the process of death;

- The right to die;

- The ability to die in peace and dignity;

- Not dying alone; and

- Expecting that the sanctity of the body will
  be respected after death.[8]

The above consideration lies in helping develop attitudes and behavior toward dying (and perhaps all) patients. Some erroneously believe that a patient should not be told that he or she is dying. The idea is to avoid the patient losing hope, which may hasten his or her demise. In recent years, medical training has become more focused on informing the patient. Much of the family's anxiety about telling the patient about his disease reflects their own anxiety about dealing with death. Many, if not most, ill patients are aware of the severity of their illnesses—particularly as they become increasingly ill. Not telling a patient becomes a barrier to communication between the physician and the patient, as well as the family and the patient.

Physicians often think of the patient's death as a treatment failure. As a result, some physicians tend to abandon the patient when he becomes terminally ill by becoming disinterested in the patient and inattentive to the patient's care needs. To help avoid this, the American Medical Association (AMA) has as an organization to inform and educate physicians regarding the needs of the terminally ill. The Education in Palliative and End-of-Life Care (EPEC) course is a two-day course designed to instruct physicians in end-of life care. It is designed to be taken by all physicians nationally.

The patient has a right to expect that the physician will be communicative about his disease, available to answer questions, and provide all medical measures, including "comfort" measures should the patient not wish to pursue an active or aggressive treatment. If a patient finds that he and his physician are in substantial disagreement about what measures to take, then the patient has the absolute right to be provided with a referral to another physician who will provide this type of care.[9]

Understanding the Patient's Condition and Likely Outcome

It is imperative that family members understand the patient's situation and prognosis when helping make a decision regarding the patient's care. To facilitate your understanding, we encourage you to schedule an appointment with the physician who is caring for the patient. During this discussion, we suggest you discuss the severity of the condition, potential for reversibility, prognosis with and without treatment, and implications for quality of life.

Physician/Health Care Provider's Role

It is also important to understand the physician's role and perspective in decisions regarding ongoing care and resuscitation. Understanding this role can help you gain a better understanding of the patient's condition and help you make informed decisions.

First, it is critical that the patient and family recognize that the physician understands how important this decision is and should be empathetic. The physician may say something like, "I recognize that this is your mother, that she is extremely important to you." The doctor should explain the situation, the risks, and benefits of the ongoing treatment in an objective manner. In other words, the physician can help recognize that a patient's death may be imminent if treatment is not initiated. However, the physician can also help recognize when, based on the patient's disease and underlying condition, ongoing treatment may merely prolong suffering without any useful benefits. The doctor may make recommendations but he/she alone cannot decide what to do.

The physician may also provide a more subjective assessment of the situation. Physicians are often asked, for example, "If this were your mother, what would you do?" Implicit in this question is, "What would your emotional response be to the situation, as opposed to your more objective view?" The physician may express his or her opinion while being respectful of whatever choice the patient and his family make.

Previous Health

To understand the patient's likely prognosis, it is important to understand the impact of the patient's previous health (age and underlying conditions) on outcomes. Age need not preclude recovery in an ICU situation. However, as we age, we tend to acquire more diseases, such as hypertension, diabetes, and heart disease. These diseases may have a marked effect on the survival of an acute illness or surgery. An elderly 89-year-old with diabetes, hypertension, and heart disease, for example, is much more likely to succumb from an illness than a 40-year-old without these diseases. Additionally, aging affects a person's ability to deal with serious illness, whether it be due to trauma, as in a car accident, a medical condition such as pneumonia, or in a surgical situation.

Imagine, for a moment, that a 55-year-old male enters the hospital with pneumonia and becomes progressively ill. He becomes more short of breath and his heart function wanes. He is transferred to the ICU where he is intubated and put on a mechanical ventilator to lessen the stress on his heart and lungs.. His kidney function declines and he requires temporary dialysis to assist the kidneys in filtering wastes from the body. Eventually his blood pressure drops considerably, requiring IV medications that elevate the blood pressure from dangerously low levels. After a period of time, his heart ceases to function properly and he expires. Why does this happen? How can this happen to someone who is "too young to die?"

One major component of this story is the man's underlying physiology (how his body works). We all know that a 55-year-old is older than a 15-year-old, but what difference does age really make in determining a patient's likely outcome?

Advanced age affects the body's ability to survive a major stress, such as an illness. A person who is old and in good health does not react similarly to a major illness as a young person would, even if he is in the same state of good health.

The primary effect of aging appears to be a loss of functional reserve in various organ systems. Functional reserve is that extra measure of function built into each organ system. For example, a person can function with one lung or one kidney under normal circumstances. This indicates that there is a reserve of functioning in these organs.

It is also important to understand the effect of underlying conditions. When an individual gets ill, there is a complex set of interactions that occur within all of these systems. If the insult is a minor one, the interactions are usually coordinated and the individual stays healthy. However, when the body is stressed by a major insult, systems can become overwhelmed and a chain of physiologic events may occur. When a major insult occurs in a body that is already compromised by a combination of age and existing disease, the systems can become more easily overwhelmed and may lead to increasing illness and possibly death.

To better understand this, let's look at two people with the same disease and discuss why their outcomes differ:

A 50-year-old man comes into the hospital with severe chest pain. He is diagnosed as having a heart attack. He enters the Coronary Care Unit where he is carefully monitored. During the first day, his heart fibrillates, posing a risk to his survival due to a dangerous heart rhythm. The nurses and doctors defibrillate him, resulting in a return to a normal rhythm. He is given additional heart medication to prevent this from happening again. During his stay he may have a coronary stent placed and possibly a defibrillator. Over several days, he steadily improves. His chest pain is gone and he is on the road to recovery.

Contrast this with a 85-year-old diabetic female. She has decreased kidney function due to her diabetes. She has a history of hypertension (high blood pressure) that has been treated over several years. She is also a long-term one pack-per-day smoker. She too enters the hospital with chest pain, is diagnosed as having a heart attack, and is admitted to the Coronary Care Unit. She too may have a coronary stent placed. During the first day, she suffers from shortness of breath. Her doctor reviews her case and finds that she is developing Congestive Heart Failure (CHF). He gives her medication to remove the fluid from her lungs and help her heart function more effectively. She fails to respond adequately to the medication. In addition, her blood pressure becomes low. She is given medication to raise her blood pressure. Despite increasing doses of medication, her blood pressure continues to be low. She continues to exhibit shortness of breath and the level of oxygen in her blood falls. She is intubated and connected to a mechanical ventilator. The ventilator makes breathing easier for her and allows a high concentration of oxygen to be administered, but her blood pressure continues to be low, and her urine output drops. She puts out less and less urine per hour, indicating that her kidney function has diminished. She continues in this state for several hours. After a period of time, her heart fibrillates. She is defibrillated, but the heart does not return to a normal rhythm and eventually stops beating.

Accepting the fact that no two people ever have exactly the same disease, it is important to understand why the outcomes of these two patients are likely different. One major difference is that the people affected had different age and health status. The first patient, though somewhat advanced in age, is basically healthy. The second patient has the disadvantage of being older and also has several underlying diseases, which significantly affect her body. Thus, when faced with a major illness, a cascade of events resulted in her body being increasingly injured. Like a house of cards falling, the failure of one system results in the failure of another system until nothing can function properly. This syndrome is called MODS (Multiple Organ Dysfunction Syndrome).

Now that you have a basic understanding of how advanced age and health status can affect patient outcomes, let's discuss a number of diseases which are prevalent in the United States. Please note that this is not intended to be an all-inclusive list; instead, it provides a starting point for understanding the conditions that our loved ones may have when a life-threatening illness occurs. The following medical problems can all have a major influence on survival from a medical illness or a surgical procedure:

Diabetes

Diabetes is an extremely common disease. It affects approximately 10% of the U.S. population. Approximately 25% of Americans 65 or older have diabetes. In recent times, diabetes has become an epidemic in America and much of the Western world. There are two "types" of diabetes: Type I, which tends to occur in young people, and Type II (sometimes referred to as Adult Onset Diabetes), which is generally a disease of older individuals. Both are characterized by elevated blood sugar; however, this elevated blood sugar is merely the tip of the iceberg. Diabetes makes you age very poorly and undoubtedly shortens the lifespan of many of its victims. Many parts of the body are adversely affected, including but not limited to: the heart and arteries to the brain and extremities, causing strokes and heart attacks; the eyes, causing vision loss; and the kidneys, causing serious kidney disease and neuropathy.

Type I Diabetes is a disease of the pancreas. These patients are young and invariably have a lifetime of dealing with this disease and its complications. Type II Diabetes is a disease of insulin resistance. These patients are usually older and don't respond to or use insulin as well as they should. They often don't make enough insulin. Both types of diabetes damage blood vessels by accelerating the development of arteriosclerosis throughout the body as well as adversely affecting the smaller blood vessels. This is why we often see patients develop gangrene and loss of toes and feet even if their pulses are still good.

Hypertension

Hypertension, the term for high blood pressure, is a significant medical problem in the American population. It tends to increase with age and may be compounded by excess body weight. High blood pressure also exerts its effects on the vascular system and the heart. People with high blood pressure develop congestive heart failure much more easily than those with normal blood pressure. Hypertension also makes the vessels of the heart more vulnerable to arteriosclerosis, narrowing, and subsequent damage like a heart attack. Hypertension also affects the kidneys, where the damage to blood vessels decreases the kidney's ability to keep the body functioning optimally. Hypertension is a major cause of vascular injury to the brain and is associated with a higher incidence of strokes, and, more devastatingly, cerebral hemorrhage (the rupture of a blood vessel bleeding into the brain).

Arteriosclerosis

Arteriosclerosis is literally scarring of the arteries. Arteriosclerosis consists of the development of "plaques" on the blood vessels, primarily the arteries. These plaques are a collection of cells laden with fat and cholesterol. They may eventually calcify (calcium may be deposited in them). They may also become covered with a layer of the same cells that line the arteries. They damage the system in several ways. The most obvious way is that they clog the artery, impeding blood flow. They also make the artery less able to dilate and contract in response to stress. They may also weaken the wall of the artery, resulting in an aneurysm or a thinned out dilation of the artery with the potential for rupture. Finally, they serve as a basis for a clot to form (a thrombosis). When a clot forms on the surface of a ruptured plaque in a coronary artery, the clot may block the vessel, causing a "heart attack" or myocardial infarction (MI). Consequently, the muscle tissue of the heart that is supplied by that artery dies.

Stroke

A stroke occurs when a blood vessel in the brain becomes blocked, causing death to the tissues in the area of the brain supplied by that vessel. Two major causes of stroke are cerebral hemorrhage and arterial blockage. A hemorrhage is an actual rupture of a blood vessel, resulting in bleeding into the brain tissue. This is often associated with hypertension, which weakens the integrity of the vessel after a long period of time. A vessel can be blocked by a clot, much like a coronary artery is blocked in a heart attack. The sources of these clots are primarily twofold: The first is atherosclerotic plaques in the great vessels supplying the brain. Small pieces of cholesterol may break off from a clot and pass into the brain temporarily or permanently, damaging a brain area. The second source is from the heart. This can either be from an abnormal heartbeat (atrial fibrillation) or from a clot formed during a heart attack.

Cancer

In all cancers, a type of cell has lost its ability to behave. It fails to stop growing or dividing in response to the normal body control mechanisms. It is, however, a misconception to consider all cancers as one disease. Each type of cancer has its own unique style. The most benign of cancers, such as basal cell cancer of the skin, do not "metastasize" or spread at a distance from the original tumor. Other cancers spread through the blood or through the lymph channels.

The ravages of cancer are caused by several mechanisms. The tumor itself seems to possess various metabolic characteristics, making a patient likely to lose weight. The malignant cells somehow consume all the nourishment, depriving healthy cells, especially muscle, of necessary nutrients. This results in severe weight loss. Moreover, cancer may cause damage due to its physical nature. A brain tumor, for example, may cause death simply because its size compresses the brain tissue. While cancer can affect people of all ages, it is certainly more common in people over 50. The reasons for this are largely unknown and constitute a totally different discussion. These cancers include but are not limited to lung cancer, oral cancer, stomach, pancreatic, liver and colon cancer, prostate cancer, ovarian cancer, uterine cancer, and melanoma.

Liver Failure

The liver performs a multiplicity of functions. When it fails, all of these functions are affected. It loses its ability to detoxify waste, resulting in hepatic encephalopathy (brain poisoning). The liver may also lose its ability to produce albumin and globulin (circulating proteins in the blood, which fight off infection and maintain the osmotic pressure in the blood stream). Loss of these proteins may result in fluid leaking out into the surrounding tissues. Furthermore, it may not store glucose as glycogen, depleting body energy stores. When the liver fails, the ability to metabolize bile pigments is impaired, resulting in elevated bile in the bloodstream and the appearance of jaundice.

Smoking

While smoking itself is not a true "disease", it has profound effects on the body's ability to handle disease. The major effect of smoking is through nicotine, one of the major chemicals in cigarette smoke. Nicotine constricts blood vessels. Prolonged exposure to nicotine results in significant damage to blood vessels in the way that hypertension or diabetes affects blood vessels. The blood vessels of a long-term smoker may have a much higher degree of arteriosclerosis than a nonsmoker of similar age. Inhaled smoke also damages lung tissue. It may damage the major airways (the bronchi), leading to chronic cough and inhibiting the lung's ability to clear itself of waste or debris. It may damage the alveoli, the small air sacs that communicate with blood vessels, damaging their ability to exchange air effectively. This is in addition to the increased risk for development of lung cancer. Smokers also seem to have less ability to fight off any infection. The end result is COPD (emphysema).

Excessive Alcohol Use

Long-term abuse of alcohol leads to liver damage and cirrhosis.. Cirrhosis can result in varicosities (dilated, thin-walled veins similar to varicose veins in the legs). These varicosities in the distal esophagus may rupture, causing severe and often fatal hemorrhage. Untreated Hepatitis C can also lead to cirrhosis.

Psychiatric Issues/Stress

Mental illness, depression, and stress are all very common and take their toll on people. None are good for the mind, body or soul.

Aging

As we age every part of our bodies deteriorates, declines and loses function. Sorry folks, this is just part of life.

A brief summary with a few examples….

Cardiovascular System

Over time our heart function declines-there are many conditions that cause and accelerate this, such as hypertension, coronary disease, cardiomyopathy, valvular heart disease like aortic stenosis, conduction disorders (irregular heart beat), such as atrial fibrillation and other less common conditions.

In addition, our arteries that supply blood and oxygen to all the important body parts also decline over time and this includes all the arteries in our body- coronary, cerebral, kidney, intestinal and circulation to the extremities. Several well-known diseases promote early deterioration of these arteries including smoking, diabetes, high blood pressure, high cholesterol and family history. The arteries become narrowed (atherosclerosis) and can become blocked resulting in a heart attack or stroke or loss of a leg.

Pulmonary system

Our lungs that are responsible for getting oxygen into our bodies and getting carbon dioxide out of our bodies are also sadly prone to decline with age. Loss of elasticity is common with aging. Many other conditions and habits also contribute to decline in lung function. These include smoking, which leads to COPD (emphysema). Others include asthma, pulmonary fibrosis (lung scarring),and pulmonary embolism.

Genitourinary system

Our genitals are not the same at age 70 as they are at age 20. Menopause is a reflection of ovarian failure. In men, erectile dysfunction is often the order of the day—prostates enlarge and urination that was previously taken for granted, can become slow and/or painful, becoming a problem.

Hypertension and diabetes take their toll on the kidneys and a significant number of people over 65 have chronic kidney disease sometimes requiring dialysis.

Hepatic system

There are several conditions/diseases that can damage the liver resulting in cirrhosis which can shorten life. Common ones are alcohol abuse and hepatitis C.

Immune System

We count on our immunity to help us recover from many infections. As we age, our immunity declines. An eighty-year-old is much more likely to die from a severe infection than someone in their 20s, even with proper treatment.

Nervous System

This crucial part of our body unfortunately is most prone to the effects of aging. Dementia, including Alzheimer's, affects so many people as early as 50 and there is no cure. Moderate decline in cognitive function and memory are both extremely common in the elderly. Other parts of our brain that control gait (ability to walk) and fine motor skills also take a hit. Strokes are more common in older people and can result in permanent one-sided paralysis and loss of speech. Peripheral neuropathy (loss of feeling in hands and feet), very common in diabetes, is an issue afflicting many older people.

Skin

Also known as the integumentary system, skin has several functions, including keeping us cool and regulating body temperature in hot weather thanks to sweat glands. Skin undergoes degenerative changes that are well known to most of us. Skin that was elastic in our 20s becomes less elastic, we develop wrinkles, skin becomes thin and friable and skin cancers like basal cell and squamous cell (rarely life-threatening) and melanoma (often lethal) become more common. And for many guys, "hair failure," also known as baldness, takes over.

Hearing

Hearing loss requiring hearing aids... enough said....

Musculoskeletal System (Bones, Joints, muscles)

Our bones become more brittle with age (osteopenia and osteoporosis), afflicting women more than men. Fairly minor falls can result in fractures of the wrist, shoulder and hip. Spontaneous compression fractures of the vertebrae are also very common, which is why some people become "shorter with age"

The joints degenerate (degenerative joint disease or DJD), especially the weight-bearing joints (spine, hips and knees), requiring knee and hip replacements.

The entire spine is affected by aging causing cervical, thoracic and lumbar pain, herniated discs, sciatica and loss of flexibility.

Muscles atrophy and become weaker. This may not sound like a big deal but often results in older people becoming less active which has been shown to hasten death.

Dental health

Teeth decay and gums atrophy (shrink) resulting in extractions, gum surgery, root canals, crowns, dental implants and dentures. Although much of this can be slowed and prevented by proper dental hygiene, much is also sadly inevitable.

Vision

No surprises here—cataracts, diabetic retinopathy and macular degeneration all rear their ugly heads as we age. The bread and butter of ophthalmologists and retinal specialists all of whom are raking in the dough treating these conditions.

Gastrointestinal Tract

Most young people take their bowel habits for granted-many older people are afflicted by constipation due to slowing down of peristalsis (normal contractions of the intestine crucial for good digestion). Constipation can certainly also have an adverse effect on quality of life and many medications that older people take can aggravate the problem.

The above-mentioned includes only a few examples. The goal here is to simply remind and/or enlighten you about various components of the aging process. The good news is there's much you can do to slow down this process and promote healthy aging. Healthy behaviors such as addressing obesity, regular exercise, healthy eating habits, staying engaged with family and friends, having screening exams like mammograms and colonoscopy (to mention just a few) all make a difference.

Critical Decisions That You May Need to Make

Course of Illness

It is also important to recognize that a patient's needs may change with the course of an illness. A patient with a heart attack might come in as a "full code," meaning that all resuscitative efforts will be made. In the hospital, however, the same patient might develop respiratory failure, renal failure, and multiple organ dysfunction. These can markedly alter the patient's prognosis and may change the decision to continue aggressive therapy. In other words, there may come a time in the course of the illness where aggressive therapy is no longer useful.

Severity

The severity of the illness may also affect treatment decisions. It may be possible for a 90-year-old to survive radical chemotherapy for an advanced lymphoma. However, treatment on someone in this age group with poor health might decrease the patient's quality of life so much that the additional survival time provides no clear benefit.

Reversibility

Perhaps the most critical issue in the care of the seriously ill patient is whether the process which is causing the patient to die is reversible. A 20-year-old man who was in a car accident and requires major surgery and post-operative care may have a much better chance of survival and return to normal life than a 79-year-old man with a stroke. Conversely, the 20-year-old man who has a proven progressive crippling disease, such as muscular dystrophy, has a poor chance of reversibility.

Quality of Life

Quality of life is very subjective since what constitutes quality of life for one person may not be the same for the next. Furthermore, we all experience changes in the quality of our lives. Even Michael Jordan, arguably one of the greatest athletes alive, reaches a point in his life where he can no longer compete at the same level. Does that mean that Michael Jordan at age 45 would choose to die rather than prolong his life? Seems unlikely. People who survive spinal cord injury and are paraplegic or quadriplegic often have a reduced quality of life than they had hoped for (although they can still live very full lives). In some cases, a 96-year-old patient who is suffering from a painful terminal condition may feel that prolonging his life is no longer justified. Often people think that someone who wants to die is depressed. This is not always the case; it may instead actually be a case of realism at the end of life, rather than depression.

Additional Considerations

Personal and Financial Consequences

There is a feeling in the United States that care should be given regardless of the costs involved. The resultant reality is that the majority of medical expenditures for the elderly occur within months of their death. The truth is that it makes little sense to spend a great deal of money to attempt to extend the life of a gravely ill person, elderly or not, for a matter of weeks to months when their quality of life is severely limited. An extended irreversible illness may also have a significant impact, both emotionally and financially, on a patient's family. While patient autonomy is to be respected, one must recognize that a patient almost totally dependent on others for his care is not really autonomous. Perhaps not surprisingly, it is usually the family who is willing to "pull out all stops" in regard to the continuation of treatment. Lack of prior communication between the patient and family members, a long history of dysfunctional family interactions, and good old-fashioned guilt can influence the hesitancy to call a halt to ongoing, non-productive medical treatment. Few family members caught up in these types of life and death decisions feel comfortable considering the long-term financial ramifications.

Religious Attitudes

For many people, religion shapes how they live their lives

and, ultimately, how they view the dying process. In general, religions have maintained that human life is sacred. Notwithstanding this belief, both Western and Eastern religions have been sufficiently flexible to adapt to the changes in end-of-life care. The concept of brain death, the ability to withhold or withdraw treatment in the terminally ill, the opportunity to harvest organs for transplantation, and the permission to withhold artificial nutrition and hydration are now often considered acceptable, ethical behavior by many religious authorities.

At this time, most religions take a firm stance against euthanasia as a willful act to terminate life. However, religions often do not view the choice of refusing treatment as euthanasia. The concept of euthanasia versus withholding treatment seems to be viewed distinctly. Moreover, most religions feel that any treatment that relieves suffering should be used, even if an unintended consequence of that treatment is an earlier death. Overall, families of terminally ill patients should feel that, in general, behavior which is motivated by the best interest of the dying patient will not bring them in conflict with their religious beliefs. We recommend, however, that one consult one's own religious advisor for more exact guidelines in any individual case.

Ethics

In general, the right to die is absolute, but many do not feel that this includes euthanasia. Several states including Oregon, Washington, New Mexico, Vermont, and Montana are "right to die" states. Some will allow physicians to prescribe lethal doses of medications to patients with terminal illnesses that the patient can self-administer and then quietly slip away into a peaceful death. In all other states, euthanasia is illegal.

Certain ethicists have suggested that we have a "duty to die." This controversial idea is that one has the responsibility to recognize that death is inevitable, and that one should not subject oneself or loved ones to a course of treatment that will prolong suffering with no reasonable chance of success.

Your Options

We want to help you face death in a prospective manner so you can make a well-considered decision, rather than a hasty decision in the heat of the moment. It is very difficult to see a patient with terminal cancer brought into the Emergency Department at the last minute by a family who is totally unprepared for his or her death, conflicted regarding what treatment to pursue, and unsure of the patient's wishes and the prognosis of the illness.

Part of understanding your options means understanding how physicians define "care." In the medical world, it basically means treatment. Moreover, we consider it synonymous with kindness, giving, being compassionate and loving, and following the "Golden Rule" of "Do unto others." To quote a sentence from *Daily Prayer of a Physician Before Visiting a Sick Man*, written by Moses Maimonides: "Let me be intent upon one thing, O Father of Mercy, to be always merciful to Thy suffering children." This holds as true in the 21st Century as it did in the 12th Century when it was written.

With all the amazing advances and technologies available in the medical world, the human aspect of care often takes a backseat to antibiotics, chemotherapy, dialysis, complex operations, physical therapy and rehabilitation. All these treatments are offered and administered to patients even in late stages of diseases. The human component of care, in recent times, often gets lost in the technical part of care.

When patients and their families face difficult end-of-life and life-limiting illnesses, they deserve to consider a form of care that not only includes conventional care, but also palliative care and hospice care. The beauty of palliative care and hospice care are addressed in the sections that follow:

Palliative Care/Hospice Care

Palliative care and/or hospice are a much under-utilized alternative to end-of-life treatment. Basically, if a patient's illness is likely to leave them six months or less to live—if left to its natural course—then a patient is qualified for hospice care. Many patients live well beyond six months when they're receiving hospice care and they may re-qualify as many times as necessary. The advantage of being enrolled in hospice care is the focus on quality of life and bringing as much comfort and pain relief as possible to the patient without attempting to cure the illness. Although families sometimes worry that hospice care is "giving up," most patients who enroll in hospice do better than expected, perhaps because they receive more care than they might in an acute care setting. You may request a palliative care consult. Doing so does not imply that you are opting for supportive care only. The consult can help you decide if palliative care services are appropriate for your situation.

Palliative care has been around for years, but it has only become a medical specialty in its own right since the mid-1990s. Palliative care is an approach that improves the quality of life for patients and their families who are facing life-threatening illnesses. This is done through the prevention and relief of suffering. It utilizes early identification and thorough assessment and treatment of pain and other physical, psychosocial, and spiritual problems.

Palliative care:

- Provides relief from pain and other distressing
  symptoms, including shortness of breath, nausea,
  vomiting, diarrhea, constipation, loss of appetite,
  and anxiety;

- Affirms life and regards dying as a normal process;

- Intends neither to hasten nor postpone death;

- Integrates the psychological and spiritual aspects
  of patient care;

- Offers a support system to help patients live as actively
  as possible until death;

- Offers a support system to help the family cope
  during the patient's illness and in their own
  bereavement;

- Uses a team approach to address the needs of patients
  and their families with advanced planning, including
  bereavement counseling, if indicated;

- Enhances the quality of the patient's life and may
  also positively influence the course of illness;

- Is applicable early in the course of illness, in conjunc-
  tion with other therapies that are intended to
  prolong life, such as chemotherapy or radiation
  therapy, and includes those investigations needed
  to better understand and manage distressing clinical
  complications.

Palliative care uses a team approach. Each team is comprised of several people with specific roles. A team might be comprised of a physician, a nurse/nurse practitioner (ARNP)/ physician assistant (PA), a pharmacist, a spiritual care person (e.g., pastor or priest), a social worker, and others, depending on the particular team. The team initiates advanced planning, including goals of treatment for complex medical decision-making, such as whether or not a patient wants to die, or when patients or families need support coping with the stress of serious illness.

Ironically, many specialists, like oncologists, do not always do a great job addressing the pain and symptoms mentioned above, as their main focus is treating the disease itself. Many serious illnesses, like cancer, are associated with unpleasant symptoms; some of the symptoms are from the disease itself, and some are from the treatment of the disease. In either case, palliative care teams are experts at treating and alleviating these symptoms, thus significantly impacting a patient's quality of life.

Palliative care teams are trained to do an excellent job of talking to families about the reality of the patient's situation and addressing denial. The team will talk to patients and families about options and wishes and help them establish realistic goals of care.

Palliative care is not intended to hasten death. Palliative care is of benefit early on in the course of a serious or terminal illness. It is about making the patient and family feel as good and as comfortable as possible during aggressive treatment. Some good examples are cancer treatment and patients with end-stage lung, kidney, heart, and liver diseases who are candidates for and are awaiting organ transplants.

A certain percentage of these patients can go into remission or have dramatic positive results after getting a transplant.

In these cases, after helping them and their families through a difficult time, palliative care is no longer needed. Most patients, however, do not make such recoveries or go into remission and are ultimately transferred to hospice for terminal care. Palliative care, therefore, also creates a bridge for transition to hospice care.

Surprisingly, palliative care is not embraced by all doctors. There seems to be a real struggle between palliative care doctors and specialists (e.g., oncologists, nephrologists, cardiologists, etc.). These doctors do not like "giving up" on their patients. Understandably, doing so feels like failure. These patients also help to pay their salaries. However, some of these conflicts merely reflect differing opinions on what is best for the patient.

Here is a list of life-limiting illnesses that most, if not all, physicians would agree are likely to benefit from palliative and, ultimately, hospice care:

- Recurrent or metastatic cancer

- Major stroke or brain hemorrhage with poor function

- Advanced/end stage congestive heart failure

- Advanced diabetes with many complications resulting from diabetes—loss of vision, kidney failure, amputations, heart disease

- Advanced/end stage COPD (emphysema)

- Patients already on a ventilator with no prospect of coming off the ventilator

- Advanced AIDS

- Progressive neurological disorders like ALS (Lou

Gehrig's disease) and advanced MS (multiple sclerosis)

- End-stage liver disease (cirrhosis)

- End-stage kidney failure

- End-stage dementia/Alzheimer's disease

- Other forms of chronic vegetative states from a variety of causes, such as severe brain injury or severe cerebral palsy

- Any chronic illness, or combination of illnesses, that is now life limiting

- Multiple Emergency Room visits and hospital admissions (three or more within 12 months) with any or more than one of the above illnesses when it is clear that the patient is doing poorly

A few words about palliative care for children: Sadly, the pediatric population is not immune from serious life-limiting diseases. Some of these are congenital (born with), and some are acquired. Most of these children end up in specialized children's hospitals. Palliative care services also exist for children and are available at many children's hospitals in the United States.

A physician who becomes board certified in palliative medicine becomes certified in hospice care at the same time. The two are closely intertwined, but they are still different services. Becoming a specialist in palliative care usually involves completing a fellowship (post-graduate medical training) in palliative care, followed by board certification in palliative care. Unfortunately, the current supply of palliative care doctors does not come close to meeting the need for palliative care services. Fortunately, many facilities are beginning to use their palliative care physicians to informally teach primary palliative care skills to physicians who have never had formal training. We welcome this change.

Unfortunately, palliative care services are not always available. Sometimes the infrastructure does not exist. However, as many hospitals and hospital systems see the need for this, the availability of palliative care services continues to improve.

Hospice care is different than palliative care. The focus of this type of care is to make the patient as comfortable as possible during their last days, while supporting family and friends in the grieving process. It has been called a support system for terminally ill people and their loved ones, providing care and comfort to ease the pain and stress of illness and loss of life. Generally, the people who participate on the hospice care team are doctors, nurses, home health aides, spiritual counselors, social workers, pharmacists, trained hospice volunteers, and bereavement counselors. In most cases, hospice care is for patients with a terminal disease that has a physician-determined prognosis of six months of life or less. Hospice is a Medicare covered benefit. Hospice care can be provided in a patient's home or a "hospice house," and is organized 24/7 by the Hospice Care team. Hospice care also provides bereavement services to loved ones for up to a year after the patient passes away.

The following websites may be useful if you would like to learn more about palliative/hospice care. Please note that this is only a partial list. There are many more similar ones locally and nationally.

- American Academy of Hospice and Palliative Medicine http://aahpm.org

- Center to Advance Palliative Care, https://www.capc.org

- Education in Palliative and end-of-life issues, http://www.epec.net/category.php

- Honoring Choices Minnesota, http://www.honoring-choices.org/

- National Hospice and Palliative Care Organization, http://www.nhpco.org

- To help find a hospital that offers palliative care services, visit https://getpalliativecare.org

Continue Treatment

Under certain circumstances, continuing the current treatment might make sense. Circumstances should be evaluated on a case-by-case basis to determine the best course of action for each individual.

Have the Conversation

No one wants to talk about death and end of life. Most people don't talk about death and dying. Because of the finality of death, we avoid talking about it like the plague—especially when it comes to our death and that of our loved ones. We avoid having the conversation around death because it is upsetting, scary, sad, depressing, and sobering. Unfortunately, the avoidance and denial of this topic often results in unfortunate and unintended consequences.

When we see patients arrive in the ER who are dying or come in DOA (dead on arrival), there is often confusion, panic, shock, and chaos among their family and loved ones. This is totally understandable in the event of sudden unexpected death. However, in the event of an expected death (e.g., someone with advanced heart disease, emphysema, kidney failure, diabetic complications, or dementia), it is likely because the family never had a conversation about the patient's end of life or because the family is in denial over the patient's terminal condition. As a result, the surviving family is often left with feelings of guilt over missed opportunities to say goodbye, make peace, and address "unfinished business." Under these circumstances, survivors commonly experience Post-Traumatic Stress Disorder (PTSD), making the grief process much harder. Not planning for the end of life leaves loved ones in a state of panic, confusion and disarray. This results in split-second decision making at a time when proper and simple planning could have made the situation more calm, serene, and dignified.

We urge you to have "The Conversation" about your end-of-life medical wishes and decisions now with your spouse, partner, child(ren), physician, and attorney. While not necessarily easy or pleasant, it is critical. We also urge you to visit a website called The Conversation Project, founded by Ellen Goodman. According to the website, "[t]he Conversation Project emphasizes having a conversation on values — what matters to you, not what's the matter with you." Their website provides a list of questions to get you thinking about your own end-of-life wishes, as well as topics and questions to help you initiate "The Conversation" with a loved one or friend.

The data from the website[11] indicates that:

- 90% of people admit that talking to loved ones about end-of-life issues is important, yet only 27% have done so

- 60% say it is extremely important not to burden their loved ones with tough end-of-life decisions, but 56%

have not communicated their wishes

- 70% of people say they prefer to die at home, yet 70% die in a hospital, nursing home, or long term care facility

- 80% of people who are seriously ill would want to talk to their doctor about prognosis and end-of-life concerns, but only a mere 7% have done so

- 82% say that putting their wishes in writing is important, but only 23% have actually done so

Having the conversation about your wishes *before* a life-limiting illness or injury occurs is key. It can help you live with peace of mind and to ensure sound, rational, and appropriate decision-making when the time comes. Making end-of-life decisions without having had "The Conversation" beforehand can and often results in nightmarish situations. Once you have had the conversation, you can decide on the appropriate documentation (discussed in the sections that follow).

Preparing to Have The Conversation

Taking a history of personal values can help determine your approach to the end of your life and inform end-of-life decisions. It provides a basis for discussing the patient's wishes with the health care provider, the family, and the surrogate/designee for health care. It is based on the belief that advanced preparation is critical to making end-of-life decisions and that the occasion of medical crisis is the worst time to make end-of-life decisions. The goal of taking your values history is not "How do I want to die?" but rather, "How do I want to live until I die?" Below is an outline for making a specific values history form as it pertains to one's own personal values and wishes regarding the end of life.

The first part of making your own values history form reflects the preparation that has or may be made for the following:

- living will

- durable power of attorney

- organ donation

The second part relates to attitude toward certain medical procedures:

- organ donation

- kidney dialysis

- CPR

- respirators

- artificial nutrition

- artificial hydration

The third part attempts to assess one's general health, including:

- attitudes towards one's health care providers

- evaluation of attitude towards independence and control of one's life

- attitudes toward relations to others; family and friends

- attitude toward life in general (including satisfactions,

fears, and goals)

- attitudes toward illness, dying, and death

- religious background and preferences

- living environment

- finances

- wishes regarding funeral

As you develop your values history form, you can also consider how you feel about an alternative in therapy, which is a trial of intervention that allows the medical team to try a therapy and then decide if it is futile. The trial of intervention may specify the length of time after one wishes therapy to terminate or under what circumstances.

Advanced Directives and Healthcare Power of Attorney

Once you have determined your personal values history, you should document your end-of-life wishes in the form of an advance directive, which federal law requires medical facilities to follow (with some exceptions – consult an attorney to ensure medical facilities will be forced to honor your wishes). Advance directives are documents that patients can use to instruct medical providers on their care and wishes when a patient can no longer make decisions due to incapacity. It is our belief that every patient should have an advance directive before becoming ill, and we encourage you to consult an attorney to explain what advance directives can do to preserve your end-of-life decisions and to help you draft your advance directives. However, we have provided a simplified explanation of types of advance directives below. Please note that the below is not legal advice, and that you should check with an attorney before drafting your advance directives.

Healthcare Powers of Attorney: this document gives the power of decision-making for the patient to another person should the individual be unable to make his/her own decision due to lack of capacity.

Again, this does not constitute legal advice and you should consult an attorney for help with Healthcare Power of Attorney.

There are many benefits of an advance directives and Healthcare Powers of Attorney. The main benefit is autonomy. A person can, by executing an advance directive, maintain their personal autonomy even if they are incapable of participating at the time it is used. "I don't want any heroics" can actually occur when the patient is no longer in the position to say that or think it. Another important benefit is that patients can make their wishes known. The families of a terminally ill patient often act to preserve a patient's life more than the patient would wish. By executing an advance directive, the patient's wishes are more explicitly known.

An advanced directive and Healthcare Power of Attorney also assists the health care provider in complying with the patient's wishes. In our litigious society, the physician's concern may not only be for the patient's wishes because the physician may also fear lawsuits and other repercussions should he/she not do "everything possible" for the patient. If the patient's wishes are known, such as in the form of an advance directive, the physician will have a much easier time not instituting life-sustaining treatments simply to avoid a lawsuit.

Advanced directives and Healthcare Powers of Attorney documents also relieve the family of the burden of decision-making.

Even if the patient has clearly expressed his wishes regarding terminal care, there may be confusion among family regarding what constitutes "heroics," how long the patient would want to live under certain circumstances, and on what terms the patient would want to continue his existence. By elucidating his wishes on paper via advance directive, there will likely be less confusion for the family who has to act on those wishes.

Advance directives and Healthcare Powers of Attorney documents can also help avoid disputes. The drafting and execution of an advance directive may clarify the wishes of the patient and help to avoid costly and painful appeals to the courts. In addition, they can help ease the burden on the dying patient. Making a decision in advance regarding the kind of care that one wishes for in the terminal stage of an illness may spare the patient having to discuss this when his/her death is imminent.

Finally, advanced directives and Healthcare Power of Attorney documents can help with cost containment. It is estimated that 30% of what Medicare pays each year goes to care for 5-6% of Medicare subscribers who are dying within that year. This argument is not compelling for patients or families facing a terminal illness. However, it does argue for much closer scrutiny as a society, on what medical treatments are actually beneficial and what turn out to be both expensive and only superficial.

Advanced directives and Healthcare Power of Attorney documents require advanced planning and constant updating as your condition and wishes change. As discussed previously, many people do not have advance directives because they do not want to be reminded of their mortality. Additionally, many physicians are reluctant to discuss advance directives with their patients because of their ethical or religious beliefs, their own fears, or because they worry that doing so may impede a patient's recovery from an ill-ness. Finally, many feel that financial considerations have no place in a discussion of patient mortality. Despite these barriers, advance directives and Healthcare Power of Attorney documents are vital to preserving your decisions and wishes if you become incapaci-tated. Again, consult an attorney to ensure that your advance directives and Healthcare Power of Attorney documents are valid and enforceable.

CHAPTER 3

What to Expect

Psychological Aspects of Death

The way an individual relates to an illness and the way it affects his interactions with people is critical in making decisions regarding treatment. It has been suggested that we learn not only how to live, but also how to die.[13] Understanding the psycho-social aspects of dying is as critical as the biological aspects.

Elisabeth Kubler-Ross, a physician, revolutionized the approach and understanding of American medical personnel to the psychological aspects of death in her book, *On Death and Dying*.[14] She classified the patient's response to terminal illness in several stages: denial, anger, bargaining, depression, and acceptance. We can also validate from our own personal experiences that these are totally normal feelings when a loved one becomes ill with a terminal illness.

Denial

Denial is the choice or inability to accept that an illness is terminal. Death, which may be accepted as theoretically inevitable, suddenly or gradually becomes actual. Depending on the psychological makeup of the individual, there may be an inability or unwillingness to accept this fact. Individuals have various attitudes towards life itself, ranging from those to whom death is unthinkable, to those who find a certain relief in knowing that it is imminent. Families may be similarly affected. There are families who choose to disbelieve any terminal diagnosis, just as there are families who are prepared for the worst.

Anger-Bargaining

Anger is a natural reaction to something that is toxic or destructive, such as a fight, an argument, the denial of a wish. The direction of the anger may be as individual as the person involved. One may be angry at oneself, asking, for example, "Why did I continue to smoke?" One can be angry at the messenger, asking, "The stupid doctors, what do they know?" One may also be angry with God. "How can God do this to me?"

Bargaining involves a greater degree of acceptance of the inevitable. It is an attempt to get some wiggle room inside the death sentence. For example: "If I can only stay alive to see my daughter married." Parenthetically, patients often remain alive seemingly longer than expected to achieve some goal, be it an extra day for a loved one to arrive from a distance or longer periods for other goals, like graduations or weddings.

Depression

In dealing with the dying process, the individual and, to a lesser extent, those close to him, go through a period of depression. This period of negative thoughts and feelings is characterized by a loss of interest in the environment, a lack of pleasure or the capacity to experience it, and biological changes such as loss of appetite, insomnia, and loss of sexual interest. This may apply to all involved in a period of premonitory grieving. If one knows that a loved one is likely to die in six months, that grieving may go on for the entire period. Consequently, after the death of the individual, the grieving process/time may be lessened.

Acceptance

The final stage is when the individual and/or his family may have a true acceptance of death. This can be a beneficial time for the individual and his family. He or she may be able to gain a new perspective on his life, resolve personal issues, be they financial or social, and come to terms with his religious or philosophical issues. To accept death does not necessarily mean that one loses hope. Hope, like worry, might give one some sense of control over a situation.

Impact on Caregivers

The development of expensive, life-prolonging technology available to those suffering long-term illnesses has also caused unintended consequences to families and loved ones. A patient who has an illness which requires frequent hospitalizations and home care can deplete a family's emotional and financial resources.

In a study where patients were treated for an illness with a prognosis of less than 50% survival in six months, the patient surviving the hospitalization required family care in one-third of the cases, resulting in a family member having to quit work or make a major lifestyle change in 20% of the cases. One third of families lost all of their savings and 30% lost a major source of income.[15]

Similarly, "over 12 million adults have left their jobs or cut back or retired prematurely to care for aging parents when paid care was unaffordable."

The Opportunities

Dying is a process for the patient and his/her loved ones. Knowledge and preparation can help make this process a meaningful one. Victor Frankel, in his book "*Man's Search for Meaning*," feels that what sustains man throughout life, even in the worst of circumstances, is an ability to find meaning. Many patients sustain themselves in the dying process by finding meaning in it. Dying as a final chapter in a life may allow one to get a sense of closure, to rectify wrongs, to communicate with loved ones, and to come to peace with one's God.

Spirituality (without necessarily invoking a belief in God) can also help many people find a greater purpose to life. This is particularly true when a person knows that death is imminent. Kessler[8] describes five stages of "spiritual reconciliation:"

1. Expression

2. Responsibility

3. Forgiveness

4. Acceptance

5. Gratitude

Expression refers to the ability, through speech or writing, to find relief by expressing one's feelings, especially negative ones. As mentioned earlier, when diagnosed with a potentially fatal disease, anger is a common feeling. One may be able to alleviate anger by expressing it.

Responsibility is an opportunity to "own" many of the occurrences in one's life. Things may have happened in one's life that one originally blamed on others. These might include a business failure or a divorce. This represents an opportunity to take responsibility for one's role in these occurrences.

Forgiveness refers to the ability to let go of hurts and injuries (real or imagined) against oneself and towards others. Many families are finally united at the death bed or in the dying process by the ability to forgive one another.

Acceptance represents the ability to be realistic about an illness. It does not mean that one has to give up hope.

Gratitude is the ability to appreciate life, both the good and the bad times, having gone through all of the other stages. Dr. Shapiro's late wife, who died young of a brain tumor, appreciated, for example, the opportunity to spend additional time with her young family during her illness.

The Dying Process

People Don't Die of Cancer

Sir William Osler, considered to be the founder of modern American medicine, states that patients usually die of complications of their disease rather than from the disease itself. That is to say that the final cause of death may not necessarily be the same as the disease which initiates the process. No patient really dies of cancer.

Unquestionably, the disease process results in the person's death, but cancer is not necessarily the terminal event. The terminal event may be decreased oxygenation due to a lung tumor that has spread, causing breathing to stop. Some form of pneumonia very frequently sets in. Death may also result from a metabolic abnormality, or secondary to lack of nutrition or a cardiac arrhythmia (abnormal heartbeat). The terminal event in any of these cases is cessation of breathing and cessation of the heartbeat. To make any decisions related to the end of life, it is important to understand how death is defined and diagnosed, as well as the most basic physiology of death. These topics will be discussed in the sections that follow.

Definition of Death

Until the last half century, the definition of death was simple; the heart stopped beating and respirations ceased—end of story. In 1986, in part to counteract a problem created by medical progress, a Harvard Committee coined a new definition of death, known as "brain death." The new definition took into account the development of artificial ventilation and intubation, which allowed for maintaining people in a vegetative state who otherwise would have died. The new definition also established necessary criteria for harvesting useful organs for transplantation. It involved the death of the cerebral cortex, the areas of voluntary functioning, feeling, and thought. The new definition allowed for termination of care in a person who had no response to the environment, no movement, no spontaneous respirations, and no reflexes. When a patient who meets these criteria is removed from a ventilator, he will stop breathing and, subsequently, his heart will stop. This state is different from a "permanent vegetative state." A patient in a "permanent vegetative state," who may have no measurable responses to the environment, may still have sufficient lower brain function so that when the respirator is removed, the patient continues to breathe on his own and his heart will continue to beat. This patient, assuming good hydration, nutrition, and nursing care may "survive" indefinitely.

Diagnosis of Brain Death

The diagnosis of brain death rests on demonstrating two cardinal features: 1) The entire brain has ceased to function; and 2) irreversibility. The first includes demonstrating a lack of function, including unresponsiveness to painful stimuli, lack of eye movements, lack of extremity movements and loss of other than spinal reflexes (knee jerk, etc.), including apnea, and lack of spontaneous respiration. This is easily tested by removing ventilatory support for three minutes to test if the patient can breathe on his own. However, more sophisticated tests with fewer potential risks can be used.

Demonstrations of irreversibility consist of knowing the cause of damage, the ability to eliminate other conditions which may contribute to the condition, and the element of time. An EEG (electroencephalogram) is used to demonstrate a total lack of brain activity. This is confirmed by a "flat line." Tests indicating absence of blood flow to the brain, such as an arteriogram, or ultrasound scanning may also be helpful in confirming the diagnosis.

Physiology of Death

What ultimately causes vital body functions to stop? There are multiple influences: Respiration and cardiac function are under control of centers in the brainstem, the lower portion of the brain (the more "primitive" centers). The body's metabolic condition may affect these centers, causing an excess or depletion of various chemicals, such as potassium. Oxygenation is vital to maintaining body function and lack of oxygen for a variety of reasons may cause death. The heartbeat may also stop due to intrinsic cardiac problems, as well as neurological and metabolic ones.

Neurological Causes of Death

Why does a person with a brain problem die? In some unfortunate instances, death comes only after prolonged suffering. Patients with Amyotrophic Lateral Sclerosis (ALS or Lou Gehrig's disease), for example, see their body deteriorate while their mental functioning continues unaffected. Ultimately, they usually pass away from respiratory insufficiency (inability to breathe) due to weakness of the muscles of respiration. If one of these individuals is put on a ventilator, they may survive for much longer before succumbing to other causes. As mentioned earlier, there are centers in the brainstem that control bodily functions. There are respiratory centers which control the initiation of respiration and the response of respiration to oxygen and carbon monoxide. As brain function is affected from top down (from the cortical areas down to the brainstem), breathing changes. Breathing may become very shallow or irregular and finally will terminate.

The brain has other mechanisms that regulate the heart, controlling heart rate and rhythm. When these neural centers are not functioning, the heart may stop beating entirely. Thus, a patient with a "perfectly good" heart may experience cardiac arrest (heart stoppage). This is why a heart, which may have stopped, can be removed from an 18-year-old brain-dead motorcyclist, and will function in the chest of a patient with other kinds of heart disease.

Causes of brain injury and death are structural, which is direct trauma to the brain, herniation syndrome (swelling of the brain, causing pressure on the brainstem, which controls breathing and heartbeat, and ischemic damage (decreased blood supply and/or lack of oxygen causing tissue death).

Structural Causes

The brain is a soft, spongy organ enclosed in a rigid container, the skull. There is limited room for brain expansion. Therefore, when the brain increases in size, there are only a few ways that it can move. Consequently, this movement may cause damage to certain brain structures and often results in permanent damage.

Herniation Syndrome

Swelling of the brain for any reason can result in herniation towards the base of the skull. If this is not corrected, and often it cannot be, breathing and cardiac activity may stop. Brain herniation results in a combination of changes that can rapidly affect consciousness, breathing, eye function, and vital signs.

Ischemic Damage

Ischemia is a lack of blood supply (and needed oxygen) to an organ. When the blood supply to the brain is compromised, it often leads to irreversible damage. This may occur in just minutes, depending on its severity. One of the main causes of ischemic brain damage is cardiac arrest. If the heart stops beating, for whatever reason, blood supply to the brain ceases. Anoxic brain damage (deprivation of oxygen) may commence within minutes. The return of cardiac function may result in minimal or no damage depending on the length of the hiatus. When anoxic injury has occurred, the brain is faced with a secondary problem: edema/swelling. Anoxic damage can cause swelling of the brain that can compress the brain in a structural manner (see Structural Causes above).

Cardiac Causes of Death

Cardiac Arrest

How does the heart stop beating? The heart has an elegant system of cells which initiate and maintain the heartbeat. This is known as the conduction system of the heart. The conduction system enables the muscle of the heart to contract in an orderly manner. Damage to the conduction system may result in a disorganized heartbeat and death. If the atria (the upper chambers of the heart) develop an abnormal heartbeat (atrial fibrillation), the heart may continue to function but at a reduced efficiency. If the ventricles (the primary muscular lower chambers of the heart) develop a disordered beat known as ventricular fibrillation, there is not sufficient circulation to maintain vital functions and death rapidly ensues unless the patient is shocked (defibrillated).

Interestingly, the major difference in survival in someone who experiences an out of hospital cardiac arrest is whether the heart is in ventricular fibrillation or whether it has completely stopped beating. Often people who develop ventricular fibrillation can be "shocked" or defibrillated back to life and the heart may return to a normal rhythm and function. However, this depends on the immediacy of medical attention.

These cells within the heart's conduction system may be susceptible to damage in another way, too. When a high voltage current is passed through the body, the ability of this system may be affected and the heart may fibrillate or go into asystole (flat line).

The heartbeat may also be affected by the chemical condition of the body. If the normal acid-base balance of the bloodstream is thrown off for whatever reason, the heart may fibrillate. Decreased blood supply to the heart may also result in termination of the beat because the conduction system stops functioning.

Mechanical forces can also come into play. If a clot develops in the system and passes into the heart or a large amount of air enters the system (air embolism-fortunately rare), the heart may no longer function effectively. The outflow of blood may become obstructed, which can prevent the heart from pumping blood effectively Blood clots are much more common than air and this condition is called pulmonary embolism.

Direct trauma to the heart is a fairly obvious cause of termination of the heartbeat. A bullet or stab wound through the heart is usually sufficient to terminate function. Similarly, when someone falls from a height or is in a high-impact accident, the heart may experience a blow to the heart muscle that is sufficient to end its functioning. Another mechanism for sudden death in an accident is the shearing of the aorta, the main artery leading away from the heart, which can lead to bleeding to death.

Coronary Damage

Anything which impedes blood flow through the coronary arteries (the arteries supplying the heart muscle itself) can lead to heart muscle injury and may terminate function. Usually this is the result of a clot forming on the atherosclerotic plaque, causing a heart attack.

Respiratory Arrest

Respiratory arrest means that breathing has stopped. When breathing stops, the heartbeat will eventually stop due to a lack of blood supply to the heart. The brain will, over a period of minutes, become damaged irreversibly from the same mechanism. Respiratory arrest is not cardiac arrest, although the latter will often follow in short order. If a child falls in a pool, for example, and is brought up to the surface after one to two minutes, the child can be resuscitated using mouth-to-mouth resuscitation and begins breathing. This immersion or near drowning caused the child to stop breathing but the heart did not necessarily stop—although if the drowning continues, it will.

Respiratory arrest can be initiated by the respiratory centers in the brain stem, which control the depth and rate of breathing. They are sensitive to oxygen, carbon dioxide, and to the chemical nature of the circulation, as well as higher brain functioning. Any or all of these may cause the breathing to stop. Often the actual terminal event may be respiratory arrest. The breathing slows and stops and death follows with cessation of the heartbeat.

Mechanical Causes

The chest functions as a bellows. If the muscles (diaphragm and rib cage muscles) stop functioning, respiration ceases. The respiratory muscles are affected by fatigue, disease (e.g., myasthenia gravis), and metabolic/anoxic effects. In addition, the ability of the chest cage to expand is important for the lungs to expand. If a restriction in the chest wall severely limits expansion, then respiratory failure may ensue. An external restriction of the chest wall could occur if someone were buried up to their neck in mud or debris.

Respiratory Failure

Breathing may not stop all at once. There may be progressive respiratory failure until breathing stops. A patient with severe chronic obstructive pulmonary disease (COPD) or emphysema may have a period of increased difficulty breathing. During that period, several things may happen. Carbon dioxide may build up in the blood stream due to the person's inability to expire (breathe out) effectively. As the system fails, the respiratory musculature may become fatigued due to excessive demand.

Metabolic Failure

We have already noted that cessation of breathing and the heartbeat are the terminal events that lead to death. However, the general status of the body may predispose this to happen. The circulation to the heart has a number of functions. Oxygenation provides the energy for the muscle work of the heart. The body keeps the blood at a certain narrow range of acidity/alkalinity. If this changes markedly, the heart's muscle cells are affected and may either cease to function or function erratically. Certain chemicals in the blood are critical to cardiac function. The proper level of potassium, for example, in the bloodstream is critical. If potassium levels increase meaningfully, the heart may fibrillate and stop. If a patient who is on kidney dialysis elects to stop dialysis, his blood potassium levels may increase. Since he is not able to rid his body of excess potassium, ultimately his heart stops.

Under the category of metabolic failure, kidney and liver disease are the most common causes of death.

Infection/Sepsis

Infection may cause death by a number of mechanisms. Rarely, an infection attacks the heart muscle directly, as in myocarditis, and causes the heart to stop. The lungs may also be the site of an infection. An overwhelming pneumonia may result in respiratory insufficiency and death from respiratory failure. Often, infection occurs in a compromised host. A good example of this is a cancer patient. A cancer patient may have a compromised ability to ward off infection, due to the tumor itself and its effect on the immune system, or due to the results of chemotherapy compromising the immune system as well as decreased reserve .

Sepsis is a syndrome where the infection is no longer localized to one organ system but rather has spread throughout the body. The most common origins of sepsis are the urinary tract and lungs, particularly in the elderly. Wound infection is another common cause, particularly in post-surgical patients. Other causes may include any foreign instrument, such as a bladder catheter, an intravenous catheter, or an artificial heart valve.

Shock

Shock is a constellation of symptoms. Basically, shock is inadequate circulation with resultant lack of oxygenation to body organs. This may come about for a variety of reasons. The body attempts to preserve vital functioning by maximizing circulation to the vital organs: brain, heart, and kidneys. In so doing, it decreases the circulation of blood to peripheral areas. The symptoms of shock consist of a low blood pressure, rapid pulse, and symptoms that result from compensatory mechanisms, including rapid breathing, sweating and cool moist skin. Confusion may develop as blood supply decreases to the brain. All of these symptoms may abate if the shock state is corrected in time. Should the state persist, there is a point where it becomes irreversible and death ensues .

Hypovolemic Shock

When the body loses a sufficient amount of the circulating volume of blood, it may develop shock. When a person cuts an artery in an accident, and the bleeding from that artery is not stopped or not stopped quickly enough, the person loses a significant amount of blood, causing shock. If the bleeding is stopped and blood volume is restored, the shock state will likely improve.

Cardiogenic Shock

If enough of the heart muscle is not functional, for example, in a massive heart attack, cardiogenic shock may occur. The heart is not strong enough to pump adequate blood to the vital organs, the blood pressure drops, pulse may go up, and other compensatory signs may appear. Here, however, increasing the volume in the circulation will not correct the basic problem, which is poor heart functioning. Cardiogenic shock has a high mortality rate because it is often due to extensive, irreparable heart muscle death.

CHAPTER 4

Other Lessons Learned

O ver the years, we've experienced and learned a few other things about approaching the end of life:

Miracles

When we, a loved one, or a friend are faced with a devastating life-threatening illness or injury, most of us hope for a miraculous cure and recovery. It is all about our survival instinct and the need to keep on living. It's human nature. We want a miracle. When a miracle happens, we are in awe. We are ecstatic. An avid Boston Red Sox fan might vividly and excitedly recall the miracle of the Red Sox comeback from being down 0 games to 3 in the Pennant race against their dreaded rivals, the New York Yankees. The Red Sox went on to win four straight games to win the Pennant and, ultimately, the World Series in 2004, ending the 86-year "Curse of the Bambino." No one expected that comeback. It had never been done before in Major League Baseball. It was a miracle—a rare exception to the rule.

Just as in baseball, miracles are rare in medicine. Sadly, we cannot hang our hats on miraculous cures for Alzheimer's or Stage IV cancer, advanced cirrhosis, kidney failure, congestive heart failure, Lou Gehrig's disease (ALS), severe brain injuries, quadriplegia, or other terminal illnesses and injuries. While we have all heard of miraculous cases like a person with incurable paralysis who suddenly walks again, or someone who wakes up from an irreversible coma, these cases are exceptions to the rule.

While it is all good and well to pray for miracles, it is also just as important and realistic to pray for strength and the ability to cope with a devastating illness or disease. If a miracle happens? Hallelujah! But if it does not, we suggest that you use the tools and resources available to deal with tragic illnesses and injuries. In addition to palliative care and hospice services, family, friends, prayer, spiritual help, and support groups are all wonderful sources of strength and support. Both patients and caregivers should surround themselves with social support to help deal with the anxiety, stress, and other feelings that can accompany end-of-life care.

Quality of Life

Most will agree that quality of life is crucial to our existence and our happiness. We all know someone who is sad or depressed because he/she does not have a good quality of life.

We all have our own ideas as to what constitutes a good quality or acceptable quality of life. For many people, it is fairly simple: decent health, roof over your head, food on the table, an income-producing job, family, friends, and enjoying hobbies and interests. Similarly, what creates an "unacceptable quality of life" varies from person to person. Being paralyzed or losing cognitive function can certainly change one's perceived quality of life, as could being in constant pain and suffering. For some people, death may be preferable to an unacceptable quality of life.

Bucket Lists

The concept of a Bucket List is by no means a new one. There are even organizations like the Make a Wish Foundation that fulfill terminal children's bucket lists. What's on your bucket list? If you are like Dr. Molk, it might include traveling to amazing and exotic destinations, playing golf on some of the world's great golf courses, making an eagle on a Par 5 hole, or seeing your children grow up to be happy and successful adults.

Sadly, lack of time, money, energy, good health, longevity, and other factors can prevent us from completing our bucket lists. What happens if you are faced with a life-limiting illness or devastating injury and your time left on earth is not that long? You could spend all your efforts, time, and money fighting the disease/injury, but we hope to encourage patients to think about perhaps foregoing treatment(s) ***THAT ARE UNLIKELY TO HELP*** and instead do things on your bucket list with your loved ones. It's up to you—we just want you to consider that option when the time comes.

Being Spiritual

In our experience, people who are spiritually connected handle end-of-life issues far better than those who are not. Those who believe in a Higher Power and an afterlife of sorts (be it heaven or reincarnation) all seem to do better when it comes to dealing with death and preparing for it.

For this reason, we encourage you to pursue some form of spiritual life, whatever that may be. One particularly memorable encounter was experienced a few years ago with a Hispanic family who spoke very little English. Their child was brought to the ER because she was vomiting following chemotherapy. A Spanish interpreter was called to the exam room. The poor child had an inoperable malignant brain tumor and had a very poor prognosis. The pediatric oncologist had notified the ER staff that the parents were bringing her in for palliative care, just to get her vomiting controlled and to give her some IV fluids.

Many of us would immediately think: "What did this poor innocent child do wrong to deserve this cruel and unthinkable fate?" One would expect her parents to be angry, anxious, tormented, stressed-out and grief-stricken. Instead, the room was filled with an unfathomable and powerful sense of calm. There was a palpable divine feeling. When asked how they could remain so serene when their child was faced with such a bad diagnosis, the parents' response was, "It's all in God's hands. Whatever happens is His will and we will accept it." If ever there was a case of faith, that was it.

We invite and encourage you to get spiritually connected and enlightened if you have not already done so. You have nothing to lose and the end of life may just be easier to accept and embrace.

CHAPTER 5

Additional Considerations

Critical Decisions That You May Need to Make

Endotracheal Intubation

One needs to be able to deliver air to the lungs. Since the esophagus (food tube) and trachea (breathing tube) are next to each other, air might inadvertently be delivered into the esophagus and stomach if the system is not properly sealed. The endotracheal tube is a plastic tube with an inflatable cuff. The tube is inserted through the mouth or nose into the larynx and the cuff is filled with air to allow a complete seal of the system. The tube may then be attached to a ventilator, allowing air to be directed into the lungs. This system also prevents aspiration, the movement of stomach contents into the lungs. In an awake and alert person, the epiglottis usually prevents aspiration, but in a person who is sedated, for whatever reason, this protective mechanism may be lost or impaired. By inserting the endotracheal tube, aspiration is less of a concern and the airway is more likely to remain open and clear. You must be aware that endotracheal intubation is considered an invasive treatment.

Mechanical Ventilation

What is mechanical ventilation anyway? In medical terms, when breathing stops, it is called respiratory arrest. Mechanical ventilation keeps lungs functioning when, under normal circumstances, respiration would cease. It gives a patient the ability to breathe when the patient cannot breathe on his own. Sometimes it is used to rest the respiratory system itself while the energy that would have been required for breathing is used to help heal other parts of the body.

The decision to place a patient on a ventilator tends to be the crucial decision in prolonging life support. There are many other interventions or "heroics;" however, mechanical ventilation is often the most critical and immediate decision which must be made.

Ventilator Function

Ventilators have become increasingly sophisticated over the years. The newer ventilators can change the amount of oxygen in each breath, as well as the rate of breathing. Certain conditions require higher pressure to ventilate the lungs. The problem with excessive pressure is potential lung damage.

So, when is mechanical ventilation a problem? First, in the case of terminal cancer patients, the end is known. By making the decision to intubate/ventilate the patient, one may prolong suffering unnecessarily. Second, removing the patient from intubation may become a very difficult process, as in a patient with ALS. When a patient is intubated, the underlying disease will continue to progress and the patient may never be removed from mechanical ventilation. Third, a patient on mechanical ventilation who is moved to the ICU may begin the process of what we call diseases of medical progress. In this situation, a patient's physiologic condition continues to deteriorate and ultimately death occurs after a prolonged period of major treatment and perhaps major suffering for the patient and family.

Let's consider two very different examples: A 45-year-old man has cardiac arrest (heart stoppage) due to a heart attack. He is resuscitated at the scene. He has an endotracheal tube placed and is placed on a ventilator. In this scenario, he might wake up in a matter of minutes and resume normal life. Contrast this with a patient who has severe emphysema, is intubated and connected to a ventilator, but because of his underlying lung disease may never be able to be removed from the ventilator to breathe on his own.

There is a subset of patients who, when mechanically ventilated, spend the rest of their lives on a ventilator. Their quality of life may be judged to be poor, at best. Someone who has major brain damage from a car accident or a gunshot wound, who is placed on a mechanical ventilator may spend years on a ventilator in a sub-acute hospital unit. For all practical purposes, the patient is brain-dead, meaning that he has no significant communication with the outside world. These patients require extensive nursing care, often are in and out of hospital with recurrent infections, and are usually treated and returned to the sub-acute unit. These patients reflect the major suffering that modern medical technology can induce.

CPR

CPR (Cardiopulmonary Resuscitation) can restore normal cardiopulmonary function under certain conditions using chest compressions and mouth-to-mouth breathing. CPR has become ubiquitous in our society. It has become a tool that is used in all circumstances—even when it provides no real benefit, such as with terminally ill patients.

Respiratory Physiology

Respiratory failure has three sources: (1) affectation of the brain centers which control respiratory function; (2) failure of the lungs to provide adequate oxygenation due to respiratory muscle failure (this might be due to disease that does not allow the respiratory muscles to sufficiently ventilate the lungs, such as ALS); and (3) lung damage, such as severe emphysema, COPD, pulmonary fibrosis or lungs filled with fluid or a tumor. If a patient is in respiratory failure, unfortunately, the time may have come to make an important decision: to intubate or not.

Artificial Nutrition and Hydration

A spectrum of indications exists for the use of artificial nutrition. A 35-year-old female who has a ruptured esophagus due to intense and prolonged vomiting may require a feeding tube to survive. An elderly demented male in a nursing home who is bedridden and in a vegetative state may also require a feeding tube for survival. Few would question the advisability of artificial nutrition for the former while many would question its use in the latter case. The difference in the way one evaluates the two situations constitutes an area of debate for bioethics.

A distinction may be made between food and drink versus artificial nutrition and hydration. Food and drink are nutrition provided to a conscious human being, which satisfies hunger and thirst. Artificial nutrition and hydration are commodities supplied to a human being who is no longer conscious or who is in the process of actively dying. This distinction may be defined as a difference between caring for versus curing a patient. Curing is a morally neutral act[22] and may be viewed as a morally positive action. It has been demonstrated in medical literature that people who are "actively" dying may have their sense of thirst relieved by small amounts of water or ice chips. Similarly, these patients generally lose their appetites and require minimal nutritional needs, if any. Caring is provision of these simple needs. When cure is no longer possible, then a medical decision to terminate or not provide artificial nutrition and hydration may be morally justified, similar to stopping chemotherapy for a patient who will achieve no benefit from it.

The ethical dilemma in the care of the terminally ill patient is the right of personal autonomy versus the duty of society to preserve life. The patient has a right to decide his/her treatment. Society has a duty to protect the life of an individual. These come into conflict most graphically when the patient's decision-making capacity is not available. The New Jersey Supreme Court, in the case of Karen Quinlan, summed up this dilemma as follows: "We think that the State's interests (in the preservation of life) weakens and the individual's right to privacy grows as the degree of bodily invasion increases and the prognosis dims. Ultimately, there comes a point at which the individual's rights overcome the State interest."

The *burdens vs. benefits* discussion has been used as a means of justifying the decision to deny artificial nutrition and hydration. If the burden of treatment outweighs the benefit, it should not be initiated. There are consequences of artificial nutrition in a terminally ill non-conscious patient that include: infection around the gastrostomy tube site, aspiration pneumonia (food being delivered into the lung(s) with resultant pneumonia), irritation and erosion of the nasal septum (the middle part of the nostril) occurring with long term nasogastric tube feeding. It is hard to argue that these burdens are worse than the benefit, which is prolonging a dying patient's life. The argument becomes more cogent if one agrees that life involves the ability to sense the environment, to relate outside oneself. When these are lost, in an irreversible manner, many bioethicists would argue that the burden of prolongation of life outweighs the benefits, since the benefit has reached zero.

Other ICU Interventions

There are many interventions that have been developed by modern medicine that are used extensively in the ICU environment. Here are a few you should be aware of:

1. *Vasopressors*: these medications are used to maintain blood pressure and heart rate in a critically ill patient.. In order to maintain blood pressure in this instance, it is necessary to use an agent/medication that causes the blood vessels to constrict, thereby increasing blood flow.

2. *Antibiotics*: medications used to treat infection. Often in the ICU, very powerful antibiotics are used. These are also used to combat "nosocomial" infections (hospital-acquired) or multiple drug-resistant organisms. These antibiotics often have extremely major side effects that may affect the course of the patient's treatment.

3. *Dialysis*: the use of renal dialysis or "artificial kidney" may be required in the course of treatment in the ICU for a patient who develops renal failure. Hemodialysis is a mechanism for creating or reproducing the function of the kidney. It makes use of filtration devices to remove toxic products from the circulation.

4. ***Blood products***: the patient in a critically ill situation may require use of various blood products for their survival. This may include whole blood, red blood cells, platelets, and plasma. Red blood cells are the primary component of blood transfusions because of their ability to deliver oxygen to the system. Platelets can be transfused separately if needed for clotting disorders. Plasma is the solution in which the blood components are contained. It also contains certain clotting factors. The greatest problem besides transfusion reaction with the use of blood products is the possibility of transmitting an infection. Hepatitis and HIV were often transmitted until screening tests were devised to insure that the blood supply was not contaminated.

5. ***Intravenous fluids***: patients may require fluids, such as normal saline or lactated ringers solution, or a solution with glucose to maintain their blood pressure and pulse. Intravenous fluids expand the intravascular volume; they fill up the pool of circulating fluid which includes red blood cells, plasma, etc.

6. ***Parenteral nutrition***: patients may be in a situation where they are using extensive amounts of calories to combat their medical disease. At times, the patient may require extra nutrition. This can be done through a nasogastric tube (a plastic tube put through the nose and passed down the back of the throat into the esophagus and stomach), a gastrostomy tube (a tube placed through the abdominal wall), or jejunostomy tube (a tube placed into the top portion of the small bowel, the jejunem). Patients may also be given TPN (total parenteral nutrition) and/or lipids via intravenous infusion (IV).

Competency

Competency is a legal issue, so we will not go into detail

regarding competency. However, in the non-legal definition, we as ER doctors wanted to give you our thoughts on competency and end-of-life decisions.

Can a patient make a decision that the health care provider and the family disagree with? The answer is an unequivocal yes. An elderly patient may elect not to have possibly life-saving surgery if she understands what the surgery involves, what the consequences of her decision entail, and if her decision-making is rational, even if others would disagree with it. If a patient is oriented and refuses an amputation on the basis that she is prepared to die, this is a competent decision.

Special Circumstances Regarding Competency

A child's ability to make a competent decision is considered less fixed. It would be hard to argue that a five-year-old should have the right to refuse an immunization. Similarly, patients with mental or intellectual disabilities and patients under the influence of medication or during the throes of an illness may lack capacity to be competent. A young adult, for example, who presents with delirium due to high fever, who may be thought to have meningitis and refuses lifesaving medical intervention, is arguably incompetent at that time. Again, we share this with the caveat that this is not legal advice, and you should consult a lawyer about competency.

Termination of Treatment

Quality of Life

Termination of treatment decisions often involve quality of life issues. Quality of life is difficult to define. It can be thought of as a continuum from "normal" (that of a healthy individual with no apparent impediment) to the opposite end of the spectrum, where a person is in a persistent vegetative state or even totally maintained by artificial means.

One of the challenges in defining quality of life is that one does not really understand the quality of life of another person. It may be easy to look at a patient with diminished capacity, whatever the case may be, and say, "I would not want to live like that." It may be harder, however, to prove that this is true for that individual.

Medical Futility

Who ultimately gets to decide what treatment the patient gets? Can a doctor decide that a treatment is futile and refuse to provide it, even if the patient and/or his family request it? Patient autonomy has become increasingly important in decision-making. While a patient may exercise his autonomy by refusing a treatment, it does not necessarily follow that he has the right to demand a treatment that may be medically inappropriate or futile. A 36-year-old may refuse to have his appendix removed, thereby risking peritonitis and death. However, he may not have the right to ask to have his normal appendix removed without justifying it medically.

Most ethicists and courts at this time believe that the patient's right to refuse treatment is basic within certain limits. In many states a patient does not have the right to take his own life, though he may refuse treatment that might benefit him or extend his life.

As patient autonomy has increased over the years, the authority of the physician to make decisions regarding the patient's treatment has decreased. A physician may recommend treatment and indeed must give informed consent regarding the treatment. He is required to explain the possible benefits of the treatment, its possible consequences, and its risks. This has often been a delicate balance for the physician who must inform the patient without scaring him half to death. The question arises as to the physician's duty to advise and offer to the patient medical treatment that he feels may not benefit the patient, or may have limited benefits.

The following examples allow us to consider how this might play out: An 85-year-old man has terminal heart failure. He is a diabetic who has had several strokes in the past. Does this patient have the right to a heart transplant? One must consider how much benefit he might achieve, how great the risks are compared to the benefits, and whether or not this is the best way to use limited medical resources.

Futility is often a matter of medical opinion. What is futile depends on one's goals. Various goals may range from simple preservation of life, restoring consciousness; ending dependence on medical care, curing a disease, or even a return to normal life. Futility may also involve more than the patient himself. If the goal of "keeping someone alive" is simply to sustain him until a son or daughter at a distance can arrive and say his final farewell, is it futile to do so?

A standard used by the medical profession to evaluate the efficacy of CPR is discharge from the hospital. In other words, of patients resuscitated or on whom resuscitation is attempted outside the hospital, how many survive transport to the hospital, the hospital stay, and are able to be discharged from the hospital? The CPR out-of-hospital survival is less than 10%. Most medical observers would say this represents futile treatment. However, one can argue that if you are among that 1%, this is not futile.

The use of a *Values History* (see chapter on Advanced Planning) may allow a patient, in advance, to express those values that are most important to him, allowing a surrogate and the physician to make medical decisions based on what the patient would want. If a patient wants his life maintained, for example—even if his condition is terminal with no hope of recovery or even any "meaningful" existence—then it becomes the doctor's duty to honor his wishes.

Conversely, if the physician feels that this type of treatment would violate his own ethical standards, he has the opportunity in advance to transfer the patient's care to a different physician, who may feel comfortable honoring the patient's wishes.

Doctors Are Not God

Physicians are often accused of "playing God" in that they may alter the normal biological process of dying. The same argument can be made to those who extend life either at its inception or at its end. Is a neonatologist who rescues a one or two-pound infant, one who would probably die without that intervention, "playing God"? The same logic should apply to physicians at the end of life.[24]

In the Emergency Department, patients and family members often mistakenly think that, within minutes, a physician should know everything about their situation and be able to treat them accordingly. On these occasions, we remind the patient that we need to obtain a history, do a physical examination, and perhaps run some tests before coming to some kind of accurate diagnosis and treatment plan.

Doctors are not God. Doctors are people who have medical degrees. They have undergone a great deal of education and training to be good at what they do, be it family practice, surgery, cardiology, obstetrics, pediatrics, or any of the other multitude of medical specialties and subspecialties. Many physicians go into research to try to uncover the many medical mysteries, causes of diseases and their cures that continue to elude us.

Why does the body systematically degenerate over time? Why are we unable to stop the aging process? Why are we unable to find a cure for so many cancers and other fatal diseases? Is it possible that perhaps we as mere mortals were never meant to solve these mysteries? The medical profession, in its never-ending quest to find answers and solutions to treat and cure all diseases and injuries, has inadvertently created its own self-image of being God-like.

When facing end-of-life, we strongly urge you to view your doctors as mortals. Viewing them as Gods or miracle workers will often lead to major disappointment. What most of us can agree on is that God has given health care providers the knowledge and tools to alleviate His children's suffering and pain. In this sense, we do believe that we have an important role. Moses Maimonides (1135-1204), one of the renowned philosophers and celebrated physicians of the 12th century, wrote a daily prayer for a physician to offer before visiting a sick man. In this prayer he wrote, *"Let me be intent upon one thing O Father of Mercy, to be always merciful to Thy suffering children."* People continue to suffer needlessly and lose their dignity in terminal illnesses and the words of Maimonides still ring loud and clear.

Physician-Assisted Suicide (Medical Aid in Dying)

We are not recommending this as an option and are largely neutral on this topic, but it has fallen into the realm of medicine for discussion. Here is some information (adapted from Timothy Quill's article *Care of the Hopelessly Ill: Proposed Clinical Criteria for Physician-Assisted Suicide*):

Prior to the development of more technologically superior

medicine, people died at younger ages with diseases that often had a rapid course. A 45-year-old who contracted bacterial pneumonia in 1935 had a very significant chance of dying from the illness. Now, patients are increasingly able to live longer with more chronic diseases. However, with this progress has come a small subset of patients who find themselves suffering interminably.

By overturning a 1996 U.S. Court of Appeals ruling that patients have a constitutional right to physician-assisted death, the U.S. Supreme Court has made it clear that there is no constitutionally protected "right to die." In a sense, this makes this discussion moot. Nonetheless, like so many changes in our attitudes and laws, the question of physician-assisted suicide has been put on the table for discussion and requires us to at least consider possible circumstances for which it may apply.

What does one say to a world class athlete left quadriplegic from Amyotrophic Lateral Sclerosis (ALS), who will wind up on a respirator as this disease inexorably progresses? Or a patient with intractable bone pain from metastatic cancer with no hope of a cure? This patient faces the horrible choices of being in pain or so heavily sedated that he or she is unable to function.

Physician-assisted suicide is the concept of the physician aiding a patient to terminate his life. It may be differentiated from euthanasia where the physician actively terminates a life. The ethical question is that of patient autonomy; the ability to control one's life, one's treatment, the care of one's body versus the duty of society to preserve life. Many who feel that the patient has a right to deny any and all treatments still do not believe that this extends to the right to actively terminate one's life and involve another person (even a medically trained one) to assist in this effort. The argument against involving a physician further includes the idea that once physician-assisted suicide is deemed acceptable in any manner, it may be inappropriately extended (either by coercion from the physician or family) to patients whose suffering is treatable or who are thought to be a societal burden, or to the incompetent patient. In effect, it becomes a "slippery slope" with no obvious limit in sight. Conversely, those who argue for physician involvement, note that by allowing an open discussion of options for the patient, he or she may receive better medical care, and the patient may not commit suicide in a much more traumatic, or only partially successful, manner. The suggested criteria are:

1. *Incurability*: the cause of the suffering is severe, unrelenting and incurable.

2. *Adequacy of care*: the physician must ensure that the care for this condition has been adequate.

3. *Free will*: the choice must be conveyed clearly and repeatedly at the patient's own request.

4. *Patient judgment*: must be "undistorted" and not the result of a reversible illness such as depression.

5. *Contextual*: it should be carried out in the context of a meaningful physician-patient relationship.

6. *Consultation*: more than one physician should be involved to ensure that the decision is reasonable.

7. *Documentation*: proper documentation should be developed and implemented to assure that all of the above criteria have been met.

Although the United States Supreme Court has ruled that a patient does not have a "right to die," there is reason to believe that in coming years the issue itself will not die. In 2014, Brittany Maynard found herself at the center of this debate. She was diagnosed with terminal brain cancer at the age of 29, and given six months to live. She and her family moved to Oregon to take advantage of the Death with Dignity law, which allowed her to request a prescription to end her life after meeting established criteria.[25]

As of this writing, several states are "right to die" states. Some will allow physicians to prescribe lethal doses of medications to be self-administered by patients with terminal illnesses.

CHAPTER 6

Review of Concepts: Real Cases From The ER

T he following ten cases are all real life encounters from the ER that deal with end-of-life issues. Each encounter presented a unique challenge. You can use these cases to test your knowledge and reinforce the concepts presented to you.

Case #1

A 91-year-old female is wheeled in from a car in the parking lot. She is cyanotic (blue discoloration—not good), near-apneic (very shallow breathing), and barely responsive. She appears markedly cachectic (extremely thin and wasted) and very frail. Her oxygen saturation is 82% (a very low oxygen level) and she is hot to the touch. We are unable to obtain any information from the patient. Her family is parking the car and expected in the room in three minutes. What to do?

Time for the "on-the-spot decision-making" ER doctors do routinely. The choices are as follows:

(a) Do nothing. She's obviously "on her way out."

(b) One of the nurses yells, "When are you going to intubate her?" Should we put a tube down her throat and put her on a respirator?

(c) Place her on oxygen, start an IV, get a chest x-ray, make her comfortable, and ask the family what her/their wishes are.

In the above case, we proceeded with choice (c).

Discussion

While a knee-jerk reaction would lead one to choose (b), common sense leads one to choice (c).

The doctor introduced himself to the patient's son, daughter and daughter-in-law and explained that their mother likely had pneumonia and was seriously ill. The doctor also explained that because her lungs and her breathing were in bad shape, she may need to be placed on a ventilator but wanted to check with them first. When asked what they desired, the son and daughter looked at each other and seemed perplexed. The daughter-in-law, however, was calm and clear." She wants to be with John." The doctor asked, "Who is John?" John was her late husband who had died a year ago. She was ready and wanted to join him. They had been married for 61 years. Since his passing, she had largely lost her lust for living. It turned out she did have advanced directives. They all nodded their heads. They understood that her pneumonia was a terminal event and she was likely at the end of her life. They were offered hospice care and were all in agreement. At this point, the patient was more alert and lucid and made it clear that her desire was for "no heroics." Hospice was contacted. The Hospice Nurse arrived within 30 minutes and made arrangements for home hospice, which is what the patient and family wanted. Everyone was on the same page. Common sense and dignity prevailed. The patient and family were ready to say goodbye. They all seemed to understand that life does and will end.

Case #2

An 86-year-old with advanced dementia presents in the ER with abdominal pain, vomiting, and low oxygen saturation of 88% (it should be greater than 94%). He lives at home and has a caregiver. He underwent a fairly extensive Emergency Department (ED) work-up (battery of tests), including abdominal CAT scan that does not show anything that would require surgery. After receiving medication for vomiting, and supplemental oxygen, he is smiling and looking better. The home caregiver and daughter (who is his medical power of attorney) notes that they contacted Hospice one year ago, but that he was turned down. The reason(s) are unclear. What to do?

(a) Get an immediate (stat) surgical consult, as he might still need an operation.

(b) Get stat GI doctor consult. Why is he vomiting?

(c) Ask the daughter if she would like us to call Hospice again.

In this case, we again moved forward with choice (c).

Discussion

In this case, the daughter and caregiver were not in denial. They fully appreciated that the patient was approaching the end of his life but still wanted him in the comfort of his own home with home hospice, who could offer him oxygen, if needed, and medications to help alleviate any vomiting or pain. They gladly accepted the suggestion of calling hospice right away, knowing that the patient would not like being in a strange environment like a hospital. A Hospice nurse was in the ER in about 45 minutes and, after doing her assessment, agreed that he was an excellent home hospice candidate. He went home. Dignity was preserved and unnecessary hospitalization averted.

Case #3

A 34-year-old male is rushed from the parking lot of the ER to a treatment room and the nurse yells, "You need to get in here immediately!" The patient is extremely emaciated. His BP is 60/30, pulse is 140 and thready (very weak), respirations agonal (gasping), and his extremities are cool. Oxygen saturations are in the 50s (not compatible with life). His vital signs indicate imminent death. He is unresponsive. An IV had been established by the nurse and his blood lactic acid is over 30 (a very grave prognostic sign). His sister is at the bedside, very distraught and tearful. She informs the doctor that he has advanced AIDS. She knows he is ill but hopes he will be okay. The doctor asks about his wishes. She claims she is his power of attorney but does not know what his wishes are. What to do?

(a) Begin aggressive treatment for septicemia and hypotension (shock)? He had both. This would mean put him on a respirator and give him potent IV antibiotics.

(b) Start a "slow code?" Minor resuscitation to be done as a gesture knowing the situation was hopeless.

(c) Explain to the sister that the dying process had set in, make the patient comfortable, and comfort the distraught sister and offer grief support.

The correct and prudent thing to do was clearly (c). The patient died 30 minutes later in the ER. He was given morphine and made comfortable. It was clearly his time. He had other family members but only his sister was with him at the end. Several other family members called later in utter disbelief that he had passed away.

Discussion

This is an example of an end-of-life scenario that truly lacked advanced planning. The patient and next of kin were in apparent denial of a terminal illness. They either refused to accept reality or were not properly counseled by his health care providers, or both. The only part of his death that was dignified was the last 30 minutes. Had he been in a hospice setting ahead of time, the last-minute drama in the ER could have been avoided and he could have had ample time to say goodbye to his loved ones and vice versa. We urge you not to follow this example.

Case #4

A 72-year-old female with known metastatic ovarian cancer arrives in the ER. She had recently undergone surgery for a resection of invasive (that means it has started to spread) colon cancer. She is currently not on chemo or radiation treatment. She was just discharged from the hospital with acute urinary retention. She has been unable to urinate for several hours and is understandably very uncomfortable. A urinary catheter is inserted and, with dramatic relief, her bladder is now draining. Her WBC (white blood count and a sign of possible infection) is elevated, but unchanged from her recent hospitalization. What to do?

(a) Admit her to the hospital again.

(b) Call the urologist stat (immediately), as she can't pee

(c) Ask the patient and daughter what they would like.

In this scenario, we again went with choice (c).

Discussion

Her chief complaint, the inability to urinate, was addressed with a urinary catheter. It was not necessary to call the urology specialist as ER doctors and nurses are proficient in placing urinary catheters unless it is a complicated or unusual situation. When asked what their preferences were (i.e. go home or come in the hospital), it was clear that they wanted to go home.

When asked if they knew about palliative care, neither had ever heard of it. Upon learning more about it, they both smiled and said "Sounds good!" A local hospice offering both palliative and hospice care was contacted. They came to the ER within an hour, interviewed the patient and her daughter, and everyone was in agreement. Antibiotics were prescribed as she also had a urinary tract infection and she was on her way home under outpatient palliative care. She was a perfect candidate for it. She and her daughter wanted her to be comfortable at home. Ultimately, she would transition from palliative to hospice care.

Case #5

A 63-year-old female has been on hemodialysis for seven years for kidney failure. She has had diarrhea for a "long time." She doesn't want to eat and has significant weight loss. She missed her dialysis yesterday because she felt "too weak to go." She appears depressed, tired and reluctant to talk. Her sister is with her and is her power of attorney. What to do?

(a) Call the nephrologist (kidney doctor) immediately to arrange for immediate hemodialysis, as she is already a day past due.

(b) Call the kidney transplant team.

(c) Get a stat psychiatry consult.

(d) Talk to the patient/sister and ask more questions.

In this case, option (d) was selected and followed by a call to her kidney doctor. She was already getting mental health counseling and, of course, you cannot do a "stat" kidney transplant out of the ER.

Discussion

Most people who go on dialysis for kidney failure live for approximately five more years, so she was somewhat unusual. Hemodialysis is a three-times-a-week event. It was clear from speaking to her sister that the patient had lost her desire to live in spite of being on anti-depressants. She was "sick and tired of being sick and tired." The biggest hurdle for the patient to "Be with the Lord" was the fact that her husband and two children insisted she stay on dialysis treatments to keep her alive. No one had ever spoken to her kidney doctor about considering stopping dialysis. In the ER, her sister was offered an opportunity to be put in touch with a palliative care specialist. She was very grateful, as she had never heard of this before, as this had never been offered or suggested by her doctors. Unfortunately, after being admitted to the hospital, the kidney doctor cancelled the palliative care consult in favor of a consult with a GI doctor to address her lack of appetite and diarrhea. Some specialists believe that aggressive treatment is always the way to go. Regardless, the patient's sister was at least now aware of palliative and hospice care.

Case #6

A frail 68-year-old female was recently diagnosed with pancreatic cancer and liver metastases. She has lost weight and is in pain. She has been sent to the ER by her oncologist, to be evaluated for inpatient management. She had a recent deep vein thrombosis (DVT or blood clot) and is on a blood thinning medication. DVTs are common in patients with pancreatic cancer. She is anxious and tearful. What to do?

(a) Call surgery stat for urgent surgery.

(b) Get stat chest CT, as she might have a pulmonary embolus, a complication of DVT.

(c) Talk to patient and family about prognosis and goals of care.

Once again, (c) was the choice. She was also given a sedative and morphine, so she was more comfortable.

Discussion

Pancreatic cancer is one of the worst forms of cancer. The prognosis is usually very poor and has not improved much in the last 30 years. Not many patients survive more than six months and many die within two to three months. This patient was likely in that category.

The oncologist had told her that he was planning to place a port ("permanent" IV site on the chest) for chemotherapy. No discussion had taken place with her or her family regarding her prognosis and the options (i.e., possibly foregoing chemo and doing a "bucket list activity" as an alternative). It was assumed that she would go the chemotherapy route. In the ER, the patient and family were encouraged to have a serious discussion with the oncologist and to request a palliative care evaluation.

Case #7

An 86-year-old male was discharged two days ago with end-stage CHF (congestive heart failure). He returns to the ER with shortness of breath due to ongoing CHF. He is on numerous medications at maximum doses to treat his CHF and uses oxygen at home, but is still doing poorly. He has been in and out of the hospital several times in the past four months. His chest x-ray is unchanged from the one taken three days earlier still showing chronic CHF. He is frail, very thin due to muscle loss, and fatigued. He is accompanied by his daughter. What to do?

(a) Call respiratory therapy stat to start him on BiPAP (potent form of giving oxygen by face mask with the hope of reversing CHF).

(b) Admit to ICU as his chest x-ray shows CHF.

(c) Talk to patient and daughter about their wishes/preferences.

Answer (c) is again the correct choice.

Discussion

An 86-year-old whose heart is failing (in spite of being on many medications) and has very little muscle mass (cachexia), combined with recurrent hospitalizations, all suggest a poor prognosis.

The patient's cardiologist had mentioned it and the daughter is beginning to realize this and is looking for guidance. She asked the doctor what he would do if it were his father. Palliative care or hospice had not been brought up by the heart doctor. The ER doctor asked, "What does your dad want?" and she responded, "he really wants to go home." The doctor called the cardiologist to relay the situation to him (he was unaware that the patient was in the ER again). Both physicians concurred that home hospice would be a very appropriate decision if it could be arranged. The patient and his daughter were on board and the hospital social worker arranged for hospice to visit them at home later that day. The patient was glad to go home and, although the daughter was not completely happy, she accepted that her father's wishes needed to be followed.

Case #8

A 52-year-old male has end-stage liver disease. His liver is shot. He has a small amount of functioning liver left but he is "hanging by a thread." He is jaundiced (skin tone is yellow), and has likely looked that way for a while. His cirrhosis is from the deadly combination of hepatitis C, drug abuse, and alcoholism. He still drinks regularly but does attend the hospital liver clinic in hopes of getting a liver transplant—this is his only hope. He keeps returning to the ER and the hospital for relief of ascites (massive collection of fluid in his abdomen), encephalopathy (confusion and falling into a deep sleep), and vomiting blood from esophageal varices (large internal veins that can bleed profusely). These are all known complications of cirrhosis and ultimately lead to death unless a liver transplant is done.

He has been seen in the ER on numerous occasions and

admitted many times to treat cirrhosis complications. Unfortunately, the word "treat" is a misnomer in his case. The treatments for acsites, encephalopathy, and varices are, by no means, curative. The problems recur—often quickly—and the patient must undergo treatment again. His prognosis is very poor.

Today his belly is again tightly swollen (due to ascites) and he needs about six liters of fluid drained just to make him comfortable (just like last week). His daughter, who brought him in, also notes that he is also a little "off" and that the encephalopathy has come back. His legs are extremely swollen, another common problem with cirrhosis.

He is largely clueless as to his state (likely a combination of lack of education, encephalopathy, and denial). His daughter, who is in her twenties, seems to understand that her dad is not doing well and is "slipping away." What to do?

(a) Admit him to the hospital and let the treatments continue.

(b) Call his liver doctor and try to come up with a better plan.

(c) Arrange for paracentesis (draining the large amount of fluid from his abdomen) even if it's just temporary, to make him more comfortable.

Answers? Both (b) and (c).

Discussion

His liver doctor, who was very familiar with his case, was contacted. She was aware that he was still drinking, making him ineligible for a transplant and had recommended hospice care. The patient and daughter were informed about the discussion with his liver doctor and told that both physicians felt that Hospice was an excellent choice, as he also had chronic pain. Paracentesis was arranged within the hour. When asked if he and his daughter were suffering, they both replied affirmatively. The daughter liked the idea of hospice once the concept was explained and the hospice nurse came by after the paracentesis to arrange for in-patient hospice. He passed away peacefully two weeks later. The suffering, costly futile care, and ongoing treatments ended with some dignity and grace.

The last two cases are real life examples that do NOT exemplify predictable end-of-life situations. These geriatric/elderly patients are still filled with vim and vigor and a zest for life. They are, by and large, still sharp as tacks and have "lots more mileage" left in them. We have seen countless examples like this in our careers and they are an inspiration to us all.

Case #9

This patient is a delightful 78-year-old lady who was leaving Symphony Hall with some of her friends after a performance of "Carmen," a well known opera. As she was walking down the stairs, she lost her footing, fell and immediately noted severe pain in her right hip. She could not stand up or bear weight. An ambulance was called to bring her to the Emergency Department. After giving her some morphine for the pain, an x-ray revealed a hip fracture. She would need surgery to walk again.

The patient had lost her husband of more than 45 years several years ago and has two loving sons and a great circle of friends with whom she enjoys a very active retirement. Other than osteoporosis (very common in older women) and mild high blood pressure, she is in good health and of sound mind. What to do?

(a) Surgery at her age is too dangerous and risky. We will need to place her in a nursing home.

(b) Call the orthopedic surgeon on call so she can be admitted to the hospital to have hip surgery, followed by rehab.

(c) Put her leg in traction for 12 weeks and keep our fingers crossed.

The correct answer is (b).

Discussion

This type of hip operation in someone enjoying relative good health has become commonplace with excellent results. She should do well under general anesthesia as she is in very good shape for a 78-year-old. She did beautifully following the operation and was very motivated during rehabilitation. Within a month, she was hanging out with her friends, going out to the movies and opera again, as well as taking long walks and going bowling.

Case #10

He is an 82-year-old retired engineer who enjoys excellent health. He takes pride in his appearance and stays healthy by eating well and exercising regularly. He has a full head of hair and looks more like a 62-year-old. He only takes medications for glaucoma affecting his eyes, and occasionally some over the counter pain reliever for mild arthritis. He is a 12-handicap golfer (really good for a guy in his 80s). Today, he was playing golf with his buddies (he does so three times a week) when he felt dizzy and almost fainted. EMS was called and he was brought to the ER. He has a very slow heart rate—in the 30s, resulting in an inadequate amount of blood going to his brain at times and causing him to faint. Previously, he had experienced a few less severe episodes that he ignored, thinking he was just dehydrated. It turns out he has a heart condition that requires a pacemaker to correct. His heart muscle and coronary arteries are in good shape but the "electrical part" of his heart needs assistance to work properly. What to do?

(a) Shock him with a defibrillator? (like they do on TV)

(b) Give him two cups of espresso? That should jump start him!

(c) Call the cardiologist—a pacemaker will get him back to his old self!

The answer is (c)

Discussion

People who live into their 80's and 90's are becoming more plentiful—enjoying a good quality of life and remaining active. Getting him a pacemaker is commonplace and considered a relatively minor procedure. He should be back on the golf course making birdies in no time. That was precisely what happened!

CHAPTER 7

A Good Death Is Doable!
Your To-Do List

We leave you with these final thoughts. Please note that these are not all original ideas but ideas we think are worth sharing.

(1) Live every day to the fullest; you never know if it could be your last.

(2) Tell all of those you care about and love that you love and care about them as often as you can; hug and kiss them daily. (See #1).

(3) Have a bucket list and try to complete most/all of it. You will never get another chance.

(4) Get your affairs in order: your will, your estate plan, insurance, and everything related to what will happen to your loved ones after you're gone.

(5) Make peace, mend bridges, and apologize to those you may have hurt or disappointed.

(6) Have "the conversation" with your spouse or partner, your children, your family members, your physician, your financial advisor, your spiritual advisor (priest, rabbi, minister, imam or other) and your attorney. Get clarity ahead of time about what you want when faced with a life-threatening or life-limiting illness. You want your wishes respected, don't you? You don't want to leave painful decisions to others and burden them with this, right?

(7) Realize that when it comes to aggressive, invasive, and heroic treatments in the face of life-limiting diseases like metastatic cancer, advanced congestive heart failure, emphysema, or late-stage dementia, less may be and usually is better. Consider palliative or hospice care rather than hospitalization or ICU admission. Saying you "want everything done" often results in unintended consequences that you and your family may regret.

(8) Become familiar with palliative care and hospice facilities in your community. They are an excellent resource when you or a loved one face a serious or terminal illness. They provide dignity, comfort, and wonderful support.

(9) Understand that some specialists do a great job in providing life-sustaining treatment, like dialysis for kidney failure and chemotherapy for cancer. Also understand that these specialists have a strong financial incentive to keep things going. If you are "sick and tired of being sick and tired" and have had enough, it's perfectly okay to bring it up with your doctor. It's your body and it's your life. If your quality of life is no longer acceptable, it's okay to discontinue these treatments—especially when the hope of improvement is slim to none.

(10) Never lose sight of the fact that life has a beginning, a

middle, and an end. Being in denial of the end and, therefore, not planning, will only hurt you and your loved ones.

(11) If you are going to be a "repeat patient," realize that is what you are. If your quality of life under these circumstances is acceptable to you and you still have a reasonable prognosis, keep going. However, if your quality of life is poor, reconsider where you are and, if appropriate, look at palliative or hospice care as an alternative.

(12) There really can be a "dignified death." You maintain your dignity until the end, you make sensible and logical decisions, you get your affairs in order, and you spend your final day(s) at a location of your choice surrounded by your loved ones (or alone, if you wish). This equates to a peaceful death on your own terms.

(13) Take comfort in the fact that if you do develop an illness that involves a lengthy downhill course accompanied by pain and suffering, your loved ones will likely feel a sense of relief when your time comes. Yes, they will mourn your loss, but they will also be grateful that your suffering has ended.

(14) Although this book is not about preventive care, it is about quality of life. We cannot overemphasize the importance of healthy habits and rituals. The obesity and diabetes epidemic is ruining our health longevity, quality of life, and our economy. Health care in America is largely about "disease management" rather than preventive care and screenings. "Disease management" is a multi-billion-dollar industry that makes doctors wealthy. Healthy patients do not contribute much to doctors driving Porsches or living in $3,000,000 homes. Eat well, maintain a healthy weight, exercise, get enough sleep, stay positive, don't

smoke or do drugs, drink alcohol in moderation (if you drink), avoid risky behaviors, limit stress, create balance and get regular checkups, including dental and cancer screenings. These will all help you attain a longer, healthier and better quality of life.

GLOSSARY

End-of-Life Terms

(adapted from *Thoughtful Life Conversations*)

Advance Care Planning: Planning for care at the end of your life.

Advance Directive: A general term that describes two kinds of legal documents, living wills and Health Care powers of attorney. These documents allow a person to give instructions about future medical care should he or she be unable to participate in medical decisions due to serious illness or incapacity.

Aggressive Treatment: Medical treatment purporting to cure or, at a minimum, save a person from imminent death; attempting every worthwhile option, thereby possibly creating additional complications.

Artificial Nutrition and Hydration: Artificial nutrition and hydration supplement or replace ordinary eating and drinking by providing a chemically balanced mix of nutrients and fluids through a tube placed directly into the stomach, the upper intestine or a vein.

Cardiopulmonary Resuscitation (CPR): Cardiopulmonary resuscitation is a group of treatments used when someone's heart and/or breathing stops. CPR is performed in an attempt to restart the heart and breathing. It may consist only of mouth-to-mouth breathing, or it can include pressing on the chest to mimic the heart's function and cause blood to circulate. Electric shock and drugs also are used frequently to stimulate the heart.

Comfort Care: Medical treatment directed solely toward symptom relief rather than toward a potential cure; may be undertaken at any time; requested by many patients no longer seeking or expecting a cure.

Curative Treatment: Medical treatment, such as chemotherapy, aimed at curing a patient's disease or allowing for an extended life expectancy.

Do Not Resuscitate (DNR): A DNR order is a physician's written order instructing health care providers NOT to attempt CPR in case of cardiac or respiratory arrest.

Health Care Power of Attorney (Durable Power of Attorney for Health Care): A document that allows an individual to appoint someone else to make decisions about his or her medical care if he/she is unable to communicate.

Hospice: Literally, a resting place for travelers on a difficult journey. Hospice care is considered to be the model for quality, compassionate care for people facing a life-limiting illness or injury. Hospice and Palliative care involve a team-oriented approach to expert medical care, pain management, and emotional and spiritual support expressly tailored to the patient's needs and wishes. Support is provided to the hospice client's loved ones as well. Hospice care can be provided in a person's home, assisted-living residence, skilled nursing facility, hospital, or in-patient hospice building.

Intubation: refers to "endotracheal intubation," the insertion of a tube through the mouth or nose into the windpipe to create and maintain an open airway to assist breathing.

Life Support Treatment: Treatments/medical procedures that replace or support an essential bodily function. Life-sustaining treatments include CPR, mechanical ventilation, artificial nutrition and hydration, dialysis, and other treatments.

Living Will: A type of advance directive in which an individual documents his/her wishes about medical treatment should he/she be at the end of life and unable to communicate.

Mechanical Ventilation: Mechanical ventilation is used to support or replace the function of the lungs. A machine called a ventilator (or respirator) forces air into the lungs. The ventilator is attached to a tube inserted in the mouth or nose, into the windpipe.

Palliative Care: A comprehensive approach to treating serious illness that focuses on the physical, psychological and spiritual needs of the patient. Its goal is to achieve the best quality of life available to the patient by relieving suffering and controlling pain and symptoms. Palliative Care may or may not be combined with curative treatment.

Power of Attorney: A legal document allowing one person to act in a legal matter on another's behalf regarding financial or real estate transactions. Help with these documents can be obtained from an attorney.

Respiratory Arrest: the cessation of breathing; an event in which an individual stops breathing. If breathing is not restored, an individual's heart eventually will stop beating, resulting in cardiac arrest.

Ventilator: A ventilator, also known as a respirator, is a machine that pushes air into the lungs through a breathing tube placed in the windpipe. Ventilators are used when a person cannot breathe on his/her own or cannot breathe effectively enough to provide adequate oxygen to the cells of the body or rid the body of carbon dioxide.

Withholding or Withdrawing Treatment: Forgoing life-sustaining measures or discontinuing them after they have been used for a certain period of time.

FURTHER READING

<u>*Additional websites/useful resources for end-of-life conversations:*</u>

theconversationproject.org

deathwithdignity.org

departingdecisions.com

dyingmatters,org

nextavenue.org

<u>*Written materials:*</u>

Life After the Diagnosis by Steven Pantilat, M.D.

The Best Care Possible by Ira Byock, M.D.

Being Mortal: Medicine and What Matters in the End
by Atul Gawande, M.D.

*Being with Dying: Cultivating Compassion and Fearlessness
in the Face of Death* by Joan Halifax

*What Really Matters: 7 Lessons for Living from the Stories
of the Dying* by Karen Wyatt, M.D.

Extreme Measures: Finding a Better Path to the End of Life
by Jessica Zitter, M.D.

*The Unbroken Circle: A Toolkit for Congregations around
Illness, End of Life and Grief* by Reverend James L.Brooks

NOTES

1. Pear R. *The New York Times*. 2015. http://www.nytimes.com/2015/10/31/us/new-medicare-rule-authorizes-end-of-life-consultations.html. Accessed October 18, 2016.

2. Choosing Wisely. http://www.choosingwisely.org/. Accessed February 24, 2016.

3. Periyakoil VS, Neri E, Fong A, Kraemer H. Do Unto Others: Doctors' Personal End-of-Life Resuscitation Preferences and Their Attitudes Toward Advance Directives. *PLOS One*. http://journals.plos.org/plosone/article?id=10.1371/journal.pone.0098246. Accessed October 18, 2016.

4. ObamaCare: Uninsured Rates. http://obamacarefacts.com/uninsured-rates/. Accessed October 18, 2016.

5. Squires D, Anderson C. U.S. Health Care from a Global Perspective. 2015; http://www.commonwealthfund.org/publications/issue-briefs/2015/oct/us-health-care-from-a-global-perspective. Accessed October 18, 2016.

6. CDC. Health Expenditures. http://www.cdc.gov/nchs/fastats/health-expenditures.htm. Accessed October 18, 2016.

7. 10 FAQs: Medicare's Role in End-of-Life Care. http://kff.org/medicare/fact-sheet/10-faqs-medicares-role-in-end-of-life-care/. Accessed October 18, 2016.

8. Kessler D. *The Rights of the Dying: A Companion for Life's Final Moments*. New York: Harper Collins; 1997:IX.

9. Association AM. AMA Code of Medical Ethics. http://www.ama-assn.org/ama/pub/physician-resources/medical-ethics/code-medical-ethics.page. Accessed October 25, 2016.

10. Association AD. Statistics About Diabetes. http://www.diabetes.org/diabetes-basics/statistics/. Accessed November 23, 2016.

11. The Conversation Project. http://theconversationproject.org/. Accessed February 26, 2016, 2016.

12. http://www.buffalo.edu/news/releases/2016/09/047.html. Accessed November 1, 2016.

13. Nyberg K. The Learning of Death, Choosing to Die. Paper presented at: Rocky Mountain Sciences Association; Laramie, Wyoming.

14. Kubler-Ross E. *On death and dying.* New York: The Macmillan Company; 1969.

15. Covinsky KE, Goldman L, Cook EF, et al. The impact of serious illness on patients' families. SUPPORT Investigators. Study to Understand Prognoses and Preferences for Outcomes and Risks of Treatment. *JAMA.* 1994;272(23):1839-1844.

16. Knappman EW. *Great American Trials from Salem Witchcraft to Rodney King.* Detroit: Visible Ink Press; 1994:56.

17. Knappman EW. *Great American Trials from Salem Witchcraft to Rodney King.* Detroit: Visible Ink Press; 1994:467.

18. Knappman EW. *Great American Trials from Salem Witchcraft to Rodney King.* Detroit: Visible Ink Press; 1994:99.

19. Knappman EW. *Great American Trials from Salem Witchcraft to Rodney King.* Detroit: Visible Ink Press; 1994:86.

20. Knappman EW. *Great American Trials from Salem Witchcraft to Rodney King.* Detroit: Visible Ink Press; 1994:105.

21. Knappman EW. *Great American Trials from Salem Witchcraft to Rodney King.* Detroit: Visible Ink Press; 1994:66.

22. Monagle JF, Thomasma DC. *Health Care Ethics: Critical Issues For The 21St Century.* Gaithersburg: Aspen Publications 1998:280.

23. Rubin SB. *When Doctors Say No: The Battleground of Medical Futility.* Bloomington and Indianapolis: Indiana University Press; 1998:8.

24. Vernon G. *Time to Die.* Washington, DC: University Press of America; 1977:21.

25. Maynard B. My right to death with dignity at 29. 2014. http://www.cnn.com/2014/10/07/opinion/maynard-assisted-suicide-cancer-dignity/. Accessed November 18, 2017.

26. Hardwig J, Hentoff N, Callahan D, Churchill L, Cohn F, Lynn J. Is There a Duty to Die? New York: Routledge; 2000.

27. Hardwig J, Hentoff N, Callahan D, Churchill L, Cohn F, Lynn J. *Is There a Duty to Die?* New York: Routledge; 2000:56.

28. Choron J. Death and Western Thought. New York: Macmillan 1963:13.

29. Choron J. Death and Western Thought. New York: Macmillan 1963:31.

30. Choron J. Death and Western Thought. New York: Macmillan 1963:32.

31. Choron J. Death and Western Thought. New York: Macmillan 1963:69.

32. Choron J. Death and Western Thought. New York: Macmillan 1963:131.

33. Choron J. Death and Western Thought. New York: Macmillan 1963:36.

34. Choron J. Death and Western Thought. New York: Macmillan 1963:146.

35. Choron J. Death and Western Thought. New York: Macmillan 1963:70.

36. Choron J. Death and Western Thought. New York: Macmillan 1963:228.

37. Vernon G. *Time to Die.* Washington, DC: University Press of America; 1977:231.

38. Sartre J-P. Being and Nothingness. 1943:244.

39. Sartre J-P. Being and Nothingness. 1943:247.

40. Tigunait PR. *From Death to Birth: Understanding Karma and Reincarnation*: Himalayan Institute Press; 1997:102.

41. Tigunait PR. *From Death to Birth: Understanding Karma and Reincarnation*: Himalayan Institute Press; 1997:127.

42. The Tibetan Book of the Dead. Thurman R, trans. New York: Bantam Books; 1994:42.

43. The Tibetan Book of the Dead. Thurman R, trans. New York: Bantam Books; 1994:43.

ABOUT THE AUTHORS

Dr. Molk and Dr. Shapiro are second cousins. Their late mothers, Judy Shapiro-Wasserman and Sarona Borowitz-Molk, were first cousins. The family connection goes back to Poland. Judy's mother was the oldest and Sarona's father the youngest in a family of seven siblings. They emigrated to the USA and South Africa respectively before World War II. The remaining five siblings and their families perished in the Holocaust and were never heard from again after Adolph Hitler invaded Poland in 1939.

Judy and Sarona somehow found out about their connection and whereabouts years later and corresponded by mail. In 1974, the two of them met for the first time in South Africa—it was understandably a very moving and emotional reunion. In late 1974, when Dr. Molk was still a medical student, he and Dr. Shapiro met for the first time in the United States.

The two stayed in contact over the years as cousins, friends and colleagues. In 2013, the two talked about co-authoring a book on end-of-life issues based on their experiences in life and as Emergency Physicians.

Dr. Molk and Dr. Shapiro can be reached at:
<u>kindnesspublishing@gmail.com</u>

Robert Shapiro, M.D.

Dr. Shapiro is board certified in both Emergency Medicine and Family Practice Medicine, practicing Emergency Medicine for more than four decades. Through the years he witnessed countless patients receive the benefit of aggressive modern medical technology at considerable personal cost and with little to no benefit.

Early in his married life, his wife developed a brain tumor. As her disease progressed, he recognized the end was close, and he asked her oncologist about medical interventions and intubation. The oncologist advised him against aggressive treatment and she passed away at age 29. Dr. Shapiro also watched his father die of metastatic rectal cancer at age 71.

"Fortunately, my mother was able to keep him at home during this time, and he passed peacefully in his sleep." Dr. Shapiro was profoundly affected by these events and, for several years was a palliative care physician, caring for terminally ill patients.

Dr. Shapiro has numerous other interests including family, music, reading, travel and life-long learning. He is an avid UCLA sports fan (his Alma Mater) and an accomplished pianist.

Alan G. Molk, M.D.

Dr. Molk is a board-certified Emergency Medicine physician and practices in Phoenix, Arizona, where he and his wife, Laura Bramnick, reside. They are parents to adult triplets: Asher, Ariel, and Eliza.

Dr. Molk has worked full time as an emergency physician since 1980. His training was all about saving lives at any cost, no matter what. It was later in his career when his mother developed Alzheimer's Dementia. During that time, he was personally reminded of how poorly we, in America, deal with incurable progressive illnesses and end-of-life issues. His extremely painful, but ultimately enlightening journey with his beloved mother inspired him to be part of a movement that is creating a cultural change in the world of Emergency Medicine—maintaining and preserving dignity at end-of-life.

His hobbies and passions include family, Judaism, music (he plays keyboards, guitar and the accordion by ear), dogs, sports—especially baseball (huge Boston Red Sox fan), golf, rugby and cricket—humor, shenanigans, hanging out with family and friends, shopping at Costco, travel, and life-long learning.

Made in the USA
Middletown, DE
17 August 2020